Maths and ICT
• in the •
Primary School

A Creative Approach

Richard English

 David Fulton Publishers

David Fulton Publishers Ltd
The Chiswick Centre, 414 Chiswick High Road, London W4 5TF

www.fultonpublishers.co.uk

David Fulton Publishers is a division of Granada Learning Limited, part of ITV plc.

First published in Great Britain in 2006 by David Fulton Publishers

10 9 8 7 6 5 4 3 2 1

British Library Cataloguing in Publication Data
A catalogue record for this book is available from the British Library.

ISBN-10: 1 84312 377 0
ISBN-13: 978 1 84312 377 4

Typeset by FiSH Books, Enfield, Middx
Printed and bound in Great Britain

Contents

Also available:

Science and ICT in the Primary School
A Creative Approach to Big Ideas
John Meadows
1-84312-120-4

Literacy and ICT in the Primary School
A Creative Approach to English
Andrew Rudd and Alison Tyldesley
1-84312-374-6

Preface

Are you one of those people who, when prompted by the computer to 'PRESS ANY KEY TO CONTINUE', frantically searches the keyboard for the 'ANY' key? I'm sure you're not, because nowadays the vast majority of people, regardless of their age and background, have experience of using computers. Even my mother, who is well into her seventies, has purchased a computer and is now happy to while away many an hour video-conferencing with her grandchildren or surfing the internet to purchase books and DVDs. In my role as maths and ICT tutor involved in initial teacher training, I have, in the not so distant past, provided sessions on how to do simple word-processing and to surf the internet. Now there is no longer the need to provide such basic introductory training and the time can, instead, be spent equipping students to use interactive whiteboards and digital multimedia.

In terms of being an ICT-aware society, we've certainly come a long way since the first personal computers were introduced in the early 1980s. Computers have been commonplace in primary schools for a number of years now, and this is also becoming the case with other forms of ICT such as digital projectors and interactive whiteboards. However, these increased levels of both access to ICT and the technical know-how to use it have not been matched in pedagogical terms. Knowing how to use a computer for your personal use does not necessarily mean that you will be able to use it effectively in the classroom to enhance teaching and learning. Teachers and trainee teachers need to be made aware of the key issues associated with ICT and some of the possible ways of working. The use of the solitary classroom computer is a classic example. Typically, pupils use it for the occasional 'drill and skill' activity but for large parts of the week it lies idle with the teacher shrugging his or her shoulders saying, 'How can I use ICT in my teaching if I've only got one computer?' I'm not pointing an accusing finger at teachers for this scenario; it's not their fault that they have never been made aware of some of the creative ways in which a single computer can be used to support whole-class teaching. A similar picture is emerging with regard to interactive whiteboards, whereby teachers are using them merely as a high-tech (and very expensive) substitute for a conventional whiteboard or blackboard. Teachers may have had the technical training associated with the interactive whiteboard but, more importantly, they also need pedagogical training so that they can use it creatively across the curriculum.

The aim of this book is to address the issue of teachers and trainee teachers not being aware of some of the creative possibilities for using ICT to support the teaching of mathematics. I want to share with you some of the activities and approaches that I have been using and developing over the past twenty years since I first had access to a BBC microcomputer back in the 1980s. Some of the basic principles that I employed then are equally applicable today, but now they can be extended to cover a wider range of technology and more varied ways of working. This book will therefore consider the use of one computer by the teacher to support whole-class teaching, and also the use of computers by pupils, both in the classroom and in the computers suite. There are separate chapters focusing on the use of interactive whiteboards and electronic calculators, and other chapters consider a range of ICT resources which can be used to support the teaching and learning of mathematics both in school and beyond. Regardless of whether you are a confident user of ICT or a complete novice, my intention is to get you to be more creative in the way that you use ICT in your mathematics teaching. Have fun – I am sure that your pupils will, and they'll learn a lot of mathematics along the way.

Using ICT in mathematics

Teachers and pupils using ICT: right here, right now!

For one particular Year 3 class in an inner-city primary school in London's East End, the oral-mental starters have taken on a new dimension since the addition of the wireless voting system to the already well-established interactive whiteboard. The scene resembles the 'Ask the Audience' lifeline offered to contestants on the popular television programme *Who Wants to Be a Millionaire*. Each pupil has their own hand-held keypad which is used to select one of the six options, A to F. Once the selections have been made, they are beamed to the interactive whiteboard so that the teacher can, at the click of a button, display a bar chart showing the frequency of each response. The teacher is amazed at the impact the system has had on the pupils, particularly the way in which it has captured the imagination of the reluctant learners, who are now prepared to be more actively involved in the oral-mental starters. The voting system is also used during the main part of many maths lessons to promote discussion and cooperative learning. This time the teacher distributes only one keypad to each small group of two or three pupils and asks them to 'think-pair-share' for a minute before making a collaborative response. The teacher has also used the system to assist with her pupil assessment by setting it up to log the responses of individual pupils so that she can analyse the data afterwards.

Now let's switch our attention to Scotland to see what's happening in the upper Key Stage 2 classroom of a small rural primary school. In fact, we could observe this maths lesson at either of two schools that are communicating via a video-conferencing link. They belong to a cluster of rural primary schools that are exploring the possibilities of using video-conferencing across the curriculum. In this maths lesson, the pupils in each school have created a model of a three-dimensional shape and are using mathematical language to describe it to the pupils in the other school. They can ask and respond to questions about the model and the aim is to deduce precisely what it is and draw it on the interactive whiteboard, in full view of the pupils in the other school. The teachers involved in the initiative have found that video-conferencing has had a significant impact on motivation and on levels of interaction amongst pupils. The technology has also enabled the teachers in the cluster to collaborate and share good practice in relation to planning, teaching and assessment.

Meanwhile, in the West Midlands, another Key Stage 2 class is looking at different ways of representing data, using a variety of charts and graphs, but there is not an exercise book or sheet of graph paper to be seen. Instead, each pupil has a tablet PC, which, in case you are not familiar with the technology, is rather like the screen of a notebook computer. It can be used in portrait or landscape view and it has a touch-sensitive surface so that pupils can write or draw on it with a digital pen. It has a handwriting-recognition facility, which turns the pupils' handwritten work into word-processed text. In this lesson, the tablet PCs have squared paper as a background and each pupil is drawing a bar chart to represent a set of data that was collected earlier. The pupils can wirelessly beam their work to the teacher and she can quickly display any pupil's work on the interactive whiteboard to discuss with the whole class. Teachers have found tablet PCs to be more interactive than traditional notebooks or desktop computers because the pupils can enter information far more quickly by hand than with a keyboard. As well as raising levels of motivation they have also improved many pupils' handwriting, particularly the boys', because tablet PCs are unable to recognise untidy work.

Now across to a primary school in a small seaside town on the east coast of England where a class of Key Stage 1 pupils is using web-based interactive resources during the main part of the maths lesson. The pupils are in their normal classroom and are sitting at their tables with one notebook computer per pair of pupils; that makes 14 notebook computers, each one with high-speed internet access, but there is not a trailing wire in sight. Battery-powered notebook computers are hardly cutting-edge technology, but the wireless network that is available throughout the school is. It means that pupils and staff can switch on a notebook computer and access the internet from anywhere in the school. They can also access the files stored locally on the school's network server and can transfer files from one notebook to another. This means that the teachers don't have to book a slot in the computer suite every time they want the pupils to use computers in maths; all they have to do is give out the notebook computers, just like any other piece of maths equipment. This has meant that using ICT across the curriculum has become a natural part of teaching and learning rather than being a gimmick or something only for special occasions. The staff have also found the wireless network invaluable in terms of planning, preparation and general administration because they can access everything they need from virtually anywhere in the school – even in the playground!

It is early evening now in a suburb of Manchester, and Laura, a Year 6 pupil, is continuing a piece of work on the computer at home that she started at school earlier in the day. The work is stored on the school's password-protected intranet, which is essentially a website that can be accessed by staff, pupils and parents from any location with internet access. The school uses the intranet to disseminate information to parents and they, in turn, can use it to communicate with the school. Laura can use the intranet to access her work, save it when it's finished and also to share ideas with other pupils. The school has seen a massive improvement in homework completion rates since it started to work in this way and it believes that links with parents are stronger and that parents are becoming more involved in their children's learning.

All of these examples illustrate just some of the ways in which ICT is enhancing the quality of maths teaching and learning across the length and breadth of the country and what is really encouraging is that they are not just isolated pockets of innovation. You could be forgiven for thinking that you are not going to get the opportunity to work in these ways for many years to come, but your chance could be just around the corner. In fact, if you're not reading this book 'hot off the press' then the opportunity may have already arisen, such is the rapid rate of change in our technological world. What is initially just an expensive dream soon becomes a relatively cheap reality, as demonstrated by the mobile phones, digital cameras, DVD recorders and other high-tech gadgets that we all take for granted as part of our everyday lives. Only a few years ago, buying just one of these gadgets would have put a serious dent in your monthly income, but now they have become affordable. The same rapid technological progress can be seen in our schools. Five years ago most teachers hadn't even heard of interactive whiteboards but by 2004 63 per cent of primary schools had at least one and 26 per cent had three or more (DfES 2004). Within a couple of years they are likely be a standard feature in every primary classroom along with many of the other developments described earlier.

Using ICT past and present

Information and communication technology has come on by leaps and bounds during the last twenty-five years (see information panel about the BBC microcomputer, overleaf), but it is fair to say that this exponential growth has not been matched by the ways in which teachers have used the technology in the classroom. In 1982 (the same year that the first BBC microcomputer was launched) the government published a report by the committee of inquiry into the teaching of mathematics in schools, more commonly known as The Cockcroft Report, named after the chairman of the committee (DES 1982). One section of this report states that:

> There can be no doubt that the increasing availability of microcomputers in schools offers considerable opportunity to teachers of mathematics both to enhance their existing practice and also to work in ways which have not hitherto been possible.

Thanks for the memory – all 32KB of it!

The BBC microcomputer was the first computer to become widely available in primary schools. The BBC Model B was launched in summer 1982 and was equipped with 32 KB of memory, compared with the 512 MB (i.e. 16 000 times more) of a typical PC today. The processor operated at a speed of 2 MHz, whereas an entry-level PC today is 1500 times faster at 3 GHz. The text and graphics comprised a maximum of eight colours and resembled the primitive Teletext or Ceefax pages we still see on analogue terrestrial television. Programs and data were loaded and saved via an audio cassette deck or a 5¼" floppy disk drive. A snip at just £399, excluding the monitor and cassette/disk drive! Very low-spec by today's standards but the BBC B and the B+ (launched in 1985 with 64 KB of memory for £499) proved to be a massive success, particularly in the field of education, selling over a million units before they were replaced by the BBC Master in 1986. The Master still operated at only 2 MHz but was equipped with 128 KB of memory and could display 16 colours. Even today there are some of these groundbreaking computers being used in schools. Don't rush to throw them in the skip, though – they're sure to become collectors' items in the near future and sell for a small fortune on eBay!

However, the report also points out that:

> Although these possibilities exist and are at the present time being exploited by a very small number of teachers, we are still at a very early stage in the development of their use as an aid to teaching mathematics.

Twenty-five years on, Sir Wilfred Cockcroft may well be looking down from above (he died in 1999) and thinking that in the case of many primary schools things have not moved on at all. At one end of the spectrum are the sorts of school described in the opening paragraphs of this chapter and at the opposite end are schools that are not using ICT at all. In its report, *The National Literacy and Numeracy Strategies and the Primary Curriculum*, published in 2005, Ofsted states that:

> Overall, too few teachers use ICT as an integral part of their teaching. Six in ten daily mathematics lessons make little or no use of it. Where it is used, its contribution to teaching and learning is good or better in nearly half of the lessons. It is very good and

occasionally excellent in over one lesson in eight. Last year, the overall picture of ICT was mixed, with a widening gap between the best and the weakest provision. There is little change this year.

However, the report does indicate some promising developments:

Some of the most successful work involves the development of work with interactive whiteboards.

and:

The training teachers have received has had a positive impact on their use of interactive whiteboards.

So, despite some pockets of excellence and the promising recent developments in the use of interactive whiteboards, the overall picture is a variable one and the final judgement has therefore got to be 'could do better'.

So where do you start if you want to do better? Right here with this book, of course! The aim of this book is to provide you with creative ideas for incorporating ICT into your maths teaching. Don't worry if you haven't got all of the high-tech gadgetry described in the opening paragraphs; not many schools have at the moment. Those examples were included to illustrate what is *possible*, not what are realistic expectations for all schools right now. If you haven't used ICT in your maths teaching at all then you have to start small, but the important thing is that you do make a start of some kind. Go on, take the bull by the horns, give it a try, see what happens and if it works – which I'm sure it will – then make sure you tell your colleagues about it so that they can try it out for themselves. This book will give you lots of ideas to enable you to have a dabble, many of them requiring nothing more than the desktop computer that is lying idle, gathering dust in the corner of your classroom for large parts of the day. If you have access to other equipment in school, for example, a digital projector, then that opens up new possibilities. Similarly, if you have access to a computer suite, there will be new opportunities here as well. Yes, occasionally you will have to put yourself out and spend a bit of time rearranging the classroom furniture, moving the classroom computer so that everyone can see, setting up the digital projector, organising resources in the computer suite and so on, but that little bit of extra effort will be worthwhile when you see the impact it has on your pupils' motivation and learning. I can remember spending many a playtime in my first year of teaching (coincidently, the same year that the Cockcroft Report and the BBC microcomputer both appeared) wheeling a large television from the school hall to my classroom so that I could connect it to an Acorn Electron microcomputer – a scaled-down, budget version of the BBC micro-computer aimed at the consumer market – to use with the whole class. The activities and the technology were both primitive by current standards: blocky text and graphics displaying randomly generated objects and numbers for the pupils to add or subtract quickly against the clock, all in glorious black and white! But the pupils were completely captivated by this and I could see that it was clearly making a contribution to their learning of number facts.

That conveniently leads to the final point that needs to be made at this stage: the question 'why?' Why should we be using ICT in the teaching of mathematics and indeed every other area of the curriculum? The simple answer is that it can have a positive impact on the quality of teaching and learning, which, as teachers, is what we are all concerned with. However, there is much more to it than this and so the important question of 'why use ICT?' is considered in greater detail below, before subsequently moving on to the more exciting issue of 'how?' throughout the remainder of this book.

Why use ICT?

Twenty-five years ago the principal teaching resource for virtually every teacher in the land was a blackboard and chalk. This was a time when innovation meant using coloured chalks in addition to the standard white. Of course all good teachers used a range of visual aids to enhance their teaching but by today's standards these were limited. Producing handouts for pupils was a chore. First, you had to write with a ballpoint pen or type with a typewriter onto specially coated waxy paper with carbon paper underneath, remembering to press the pen or thump the typewriter keys as hard as you could. The sheet was then attached to a spirit-fuelled banda machine (Oh, that smell!), which you would then crank by hand to produce multiple copies for the pupils. The alternative, a primitive photocopying machine, was available only in those schools prepared to sacrifice the annual salary of a member of staff, such was the cost. Mathematical visual aids and resources for the pupils were largely paper-based, together with some practical apparatus such as interlocking cubes, counters, wooden or plastic shapes. The principal tool for teacher assessment was a red pen, the results were recorded by hand in a mark book, any analysis was done manually or with the aid of a calculator and reports to parents were entirely the handwritten work of the teacher.

The increasing availability of ICT over the last twenty-five years has completely transformed the ways in which the majority of teachers now work, to such an extent that even the most ardent traditionalists are likely to be using ICT in their professional role in some way or another. At every stage there are opportunities to reap the benefits offered by ICT; from preparation and planning, through to teaching and learning in the classroom, through to assessment, recording and reporting to parents. However, there may still be teachers who remain unconvinced or who are simply unaware of the benefits, and so the aim here is to present a persuasive argument in favour of using ICT in the primary classroom with particular reference to the teaching of mathematics.

The first point to make about the use of ICT relates to the nature of the high-tech world in which we live. Most aspects of our everyday experiences provide evidence of this, for example, the wealth of electronic gadgetry that we have in our homes and carry around with us in our pockets, as well as the technology we encounter when we go through the supermarket checkout, fill the car with petrol, withdraw money from the bank, order a meal or pay for a round of drinks in the pub, borrow a book or CD from the library, and so on. The list is almost endless and that's before we've even considered the world of work; nowadays there are very few occupations that do not involve the use of ICT in some form. So we owe it to pupils to prepare them to be citizens in a technology-rich world and this should start in the earliest stages of their schooling. This alone should be sufficient justification for ensuring that all pupils see and experience ICT in a very positive way, not just in maths but in all areas of the curriculum.

The nature of the technology itself provides additional support for its use in schools. Computers and electronic calculators are fast and powerful and can therefore carry out low-level mechanical chores very efficiently, thus freeing up time for the user to spend on higher-level skills. One example of this is a teacher employing a spreadsheet to analyse pupils' marks; another is pupils using a data-handling program to sort, search and graph data that they have collected. In both cases the computer does the tedious work so that the user can concentrate on analysis, interpretation and problem-solving. As well as being fast and powerful, computers can store and retrieve huge quantities of information, both locally, for example using hard disks, CD-ROMs and memory sticks, and remotely, via networks, intranets and the internet. Consequently, teachers, pupils and parents are able to access rich and varied resources that were simply not available a few years ago, and all at the click of a few buttons without even having to get up from their seats. Technology also allows the information to be presented more accurately and more attractively than by traditional means so that it engages the attention of the user. Why rely on a scruffy, hurriedly drawn pie chart on the blackboard when you can produce a more effective visual aid with a computer? Technology is also inclusive in that the information can be presented in a variety of ways according to the size of the audience and the special needs of particular individuals. Another feature of the information being presented is that it can comprise various media such as text, graphics, sounds, animations and video, hence the expression 'multimedia'. This, together with the often interactive nature of the materials being presented, captures the interest of the user and motivates him or her to learn.

It would be very easy to get into a heavy discussion of learning theories, behaviourism, constructivism, Piaget and a whole complex of other psychologists but, instead, I should like to raise just one simple fact about learning: children learn what they choose to learn. We cannot force our students or pupils to learn and it is this optional feature of learning that requires us to inspire, to motivate, to open doors and to make them want to learn. ICT can play a key part in achieving this. Doubtless we all have anecdotal evidence of how children are motivated by ICT and there is a growing body of research literature to support these beliefs. The evidence suggests that ICT can have a positive impact on pupils' levels of concentration, self-confidence, self-esteem, independence and behaviour. Although this applies to all pupils, there are particular benefits for those who are reluctant learners or have special educational needs. One reason for this is that when using ICT the pupil is required to employ different sorts of skills to those needed when using pens, pencils, rulers, protractors, graph paper, and so on. These pupils usually adapt to the ICT approach more readily than the traditional one and so have an opportunity to savour some much-needed success, thus raising their self-esteem. Their tables and graphs will look just as impressive as those produced by the rest of the class and will certainly be worthy of display on the wall along with everyone else's. Similarly the ICT approach can provide access to the curriculum for those with a special educational need of a physical nature, for example, those with poor motor control who find it difficult to produce legible work by hand.

ICT can benefit pupils with special educational needs in other ways, particularly when they are using computer-based learning materials. First, such materials often break down the skills and content being taught into small, achievable steps, thus allowing the learner to demonstrate measurable progress. Second, there are major advantages in terms of the learning taking place 'in private'. The child can work at his or her own pace without fear of appearing slow or holding back the rest of the class. A child who makes a mistake does not have to worry about looking foolish in front of everyone else and can simply have another go, usually after being given additional hints or clues by the computer. In many ways the computer can never replace good quality interaction with an effective teacher, but the instant, impartial feedback it offers is something that the teacher is not always able to match.

Research has also shown that with computer-based activities, pupils are more likely to experiment and take risks than they would have been in the past, which is precisely what we want them to do, particularly when carrying out investigative, open-ended, problem-solving activities that encourage pupils to make decisions, predictions and generalisations, and to employ skills such as estimation and trial and improvement. ICT has also opened new doors in terms of the contexts in which these skills can be developed. For example, as we shall see in Chapter 2, a spreadsheet can be used by the pupils or the teacher to model various mathematical situations that would otherwise be either impossible or too time-consuming to carry out in the classroom. ICT tools also enable pupils to get to grips with mathematical concepts more quickly and more easily than in the past. One example of this is the use by young children of a programmable floor robot to assist their understanding of the concept of angle as an amount of turning. Another example, involving older children, is the use of data-logging equipment, which provides

Assig 2

maths

access to complex scientific and mathematical concepts such as the warming and cooling of liquids and the graphical representation of these changes over a period of time.

So ICT has a lot to offer for the pupils, but what's in it for you? Well, if your pupils are benefiting in the ways described above then clearly it's going to assist you in your role as an effective teacher, but there are some additional specific benefits to be aware of. The widespread availability of ICT, particularly the internet, means that you now have easy access to a huge bank of ready-made resources that can be used to enhance your teaching. Why reinvent the wheel when someone else has already created that lesson plan, activity sheet, data file, pre-written spreadsheet, *PowerPoint* presentation or set of Logo procedures that you want to use in tomorrow's maths lesson? The government's Standards Site is a good place to start, providing Unit Plans for numeracy which you can use as the basis of your short-term planning, Interactive Teaching Programs to support whole-class teaching with a computer or interactive whiteboard, Springboard catch-up materials for pupils with weaknesses in their number work, and much, much more. The materials on the Standards Site represent just a small proportion of what is available on the internet and all of this offers the potential to save you a great deal of time, effort and head-scratching in trying to come up with stimulating ideas to use in the classroom. If you haven't started to make use of the internet in this way then you really don't know what you're missing out on, and so I suggest you put this book down right now and start browsing!

ICT tools, such as word-processors, desktop publishing packages and presentation software, also make creating your own attractive, stimulating resources a relatively straightforward and very satisfying task. You can create professional looking printed materials as well as visual aids to display on a computer screen or project onto the wall and, because they are stored electronically, you can edit and add to them very easily for future use. It also means that you can share them with colleagues in your school and, by encouraging this sort of sharing culture, ultimately everyone benefits. Making use of shared folders on the school's computer network is an excellent way of promoting this way of working. The more that staff put in to it, the more they get out of it, both literally and metaphorically.

Summary

From the teacher's perspective, ICT enables you to access or create stimulating resources, to distribute or display them attractively to individuals, groups and whole classes of pupils, to capture the interest of your pupils and motivate them to want to learn, to address the issue of inclusion by providing all pupils with access to the curriculum, to share your resources with colleagues, and to carry out many of your administrative tasks more effectively and efficiently. Basically, there are many things that can be done better with ICT than without it and this is demonstrated in the remaining chapters of this book, which provide you with a range of tips, ideas and advice to get you on the road to using ICT in your maths teaching.

References and additional reading

DES (1982) *Mathematics counts* (The Cockcroft Report). London: DES/HMSO.

DfES (2004) *ICT in Schools Survey 2004*. London: DfES. This publication is also available at: http://www.partners.becta.org.uk

Ofsted (2005) *The National Literacy and Numeracy Strategies and the Primary Curriculum*. London: Ofsted. This publication is also available at: http://www.ofsted.gov.uk/publications/

Web resources

The Unit Plans, Springboard materials and the Interactive Teaching Programs (ITPs) are available in the mathematics section of the Primary National Strategy website: http://www.standards.dfes.gov.uk/primary/mathematics/

The Research section of the British Educational Communications and Technology Agency (Becta) website provides many publications which discuss the benefits of using ICT. http://www.partners.becta.org.uk/

Transforming your maths teaching with an interactive whiteboard

Introduction

Perhaps more than any other technological development in the last twenty years, the interactive whiteboard has taken the educational world by storm and has the potential to transform teaching and learning in our schools. At the turn of the new millennium interactive whiteboards were almost unheard of in primary schools, but at about this time a number of initiatives, for example the establishment and funding of Education Action Zones, resulted in the introduction of this new technology so that by 2001 nine per cent of primary schools in England were equipped with at least one interactive whiteboard. By spring 2004 this figure had risen to 63 per cent (DfES 2004b) and this included a significant number of schools with an interactive whiteboard in every classroom from Reception to Year 6. Why this uncharacteristic rush to embrace new technology? Well, as Ofsted (2004b) states:

> The use of interactive whiteboards is adding an exciting new dimension to teaching and learning.

So, unless you've been on a five-year sabbatical, you should know what this piece of new technology is all about and you will be building up a mass of anecdotal evidence to support the claims that Ofsted and other commentators are making. Just in case you're not too sure what all the fuss is about then let me briefly explain. When people refer to an 'interactive whiteboard' they are in fact talking about three pieces of linked technology: a computer, a digital projector and a large, white, touch-sensitive board that is usually fixed to the wall of the classroom. The computer connects to both the digital projector and the whiteboard so that the latter, in effect, becomes a giant touch-sensitive computer screen. All the things that you would normally do with the mouse whilst sitting at the computer can now be done at the whiteboard, using a special pen or stylus or sometimes even your finger, depending on the brand of whiteboard. No more problems trying to ensure that all pupils can see what's going on and no need to keep walking across to the computer to use the keyboard and mouse: you can do it all at the whiteboard in full view of all the pupils.

What are the benefits?

The previous chapter identified the benefits offered by ICT in the teaching of mathematics and many of these are relevant to the particular case of interactive whiteboards. Here is a summary of the key benefits.

- Interactive whiteboards provide an effective way of presenting information to the whole class rather than having to gather pupils around a conventional computer screen.

- Interactive whiteboards emphasise the whole-class teaching strategies identified in the introductory section of the *Framework for teaching mathematics from Reception to Year 6* (DfEE 1999): directing, instructing, demonstrating, explaining and illustrating, questioning and discussing, consolidating, evaluating pupils' responses, and summarising.

- Pens and highlighters in a variety of vivid colours can be used to emphasise particular items on the whiteboard.

- Multimedia and the internet can be used to bring material to life, thus giving pupils access to difficult mathematical concepts.

- On-screen resources such as graph paper, spotty paper, tables, charts, grids, number lines, and so on provide a quick and effective way of presenting mathematical concepts.

- Animations and other facilities allow the user to rotate, reflect, translate and enlarge shapes, numbers and words to demonstrate particular aspects of mathematics.

- The on-screen 'flipchart' or 'notebook' facility provides an unlimited number of screens of information which can be accessed instantly in any order, thus allowing the user to revisit (e.g. in the plenary) material that was first presented earlier in the lesson. With a traditional blackboard or whiteboard, once the calculation, note or drawing has been rubbed out, it cannot be retrieved.

- If used effectively, interactive whiteboards can result in greater pace being injected into lessons.

- The features described above can result in higher levels of motivation, concentration, participation and enjoyment amongst pupils.

- If used effectively, interactive whiteboards promote the philosophy and underlying principles of *Excellence and Enjoyment* (DfES 2004a).

- On-screen 'flipchart' or 'notebook' materials can be prepared by the teacher in advance of the lesson.
- The electronic nature of these materials means that they can be shared easily with colleagues and reused in the future with other classes, thus reducing preparation time in the long term.
- There is a huge bank of free resources available on the internet which can be used with an interactive whiteboard, including 'flipchart' and 'notebook' materials that have been created by other teachers, again contributing to a long-term reduction in preparation time.
- Pupils using the interactive whiteboard are provided with opportunities to develop their coordination and communication skills as well as their confidence.

The points listed above are based on a wide range of anecdotal evidence recounted by teachers with much experience of using interactive whiteboards. They are also reiterated by research and inspection evidence from bodies such as the Office for Standards in Education (Ofsted 2003, 2004a, 2004b, 2005), the British Educational Communications and Technology Agency (Becta 2003) and the Department for Education and Skills (Passey and Rogers 2004).

A few words of warning

The preceding section suggests that interactive whiteboards offer the solution to many of our current educational ills, but before you dash out and start hammering on your headteacher's door, demanding the immediate installation of one in your classroom, let's have a look at a few cautionary tales.

Without doubt you can captivate and mesmerise your pupils by using an interactive whiteboard – but you could achieve the same jaw-dropping effect by looking in *Yellow Pages* and hiring the local fire-eater or human cannonball for the morning. Let's not forget that we're in the business of improving the quality of mathematics teaching and learning, not simply entertaining classes of pupils, and so substance should always take priority over 'awe and wonder'. Some teachers are themselves captivated by the fact that they can maintain the attention of their pupils by employing an interactive whiteboard (particularly if this has been a problem in the past) and so this can lead to an overemphasis on entertainment at the expense of teaching and learning. Another side effect is that even good teachers who are using interactive whiteboards effectively can fall into the trap of spending too long working with the whole class at the expense of pupils working independently or in small groups. Regardless of whether you have access to an interactive whiteboard or not, the aim should be to achieve an appropriate balance between these different ways of working during the main part of the lesson.

Another issue is the *quality* of the interaction between teacher and pupils when using an interactive whiteboard. Most people assume that the 'interactive' in 'interactive whiteboard' is referring to the interaction between the user (i.e. the teacher) and the board and doubtless this is the interpretation that was intended when the expression was first devised. However, the most important interaction is that between the teacher and the pupils. The interactive whiteboard offers the potential to make such interactions more effective but, sadly, this potential is not often realised and sometimes the use of an interactive whiteboard actually *reduces* the quality of the interaction. In extreme cases there is little or no interaction, resulting in the pupils' role being reduced to that of passive observers who might as well be watching a television programme. When the interaction is reduced to these levels it is likely that the amount of learning is also reduced and the teacher is certainly not able to establish whether any learning is taking place; in other words, the teacher is no longer able to assess pupil progress. An example of this is a shape and space lesson focusing on the properties of two-dimensional shapes. The teacher can use the interactive whiteboard to present a range of shapes, all colour-coded, drawn with precision, complete with stunning entrance animations and perhaps a few amusing sound effects thrown in for good measure. The teacher might choose to describe the properties of the shapes to the pupils or, better still, why not have each piece of text spiralling outwards from the centre of the shape? Almost anything is possible with an interactive whiteboard! But all of this is of minimal educational value if there is no interaction between the teacher and the pupils. We're back to the issue raised earlier about the role of the teacher being much more than that of a children's entertainer.

One possible explanation for the reduction in teacher–pupil interaction is that the teacher's main focus, when both preparing and delivering the lesson, is on the technical possibilities offered by the interactive whiteboard rather than on the learning objectives and the most effective ways of achieving them. The temptation is to try to incorporate as many of the 'bells and whistles' to create that 'gee-whiz' effect, when often the best option is to go back to basics and keep things simple. Keeping things simple might often mean using traditional, non-computer-based resources and visual aids. For many years, and particularly since the advent of the National Numeracy Strategy, teachers have been using a range of resources to support whole-class teaching, including multilink cubes, models of three-dimensional shapes, large foam dice, washing lines with number cards and pegs, place-value cards, and so on. The danger is that all of this valuable equipment is pushed to one side as soon as an interactive whiteboard becomes available, but this is a big mistake. The key consideration should always be *fitness for purpose*, in other words, selecting the most effective approach to achieve a particular learning objective, and if this means using a traditional visual aid then so be it. Yes, there are some traditional visual aids that can be used to far greater effect when presented in computerised form, for example number lines and number grids, but sometimes technology is not the best option. Ultimately this is a decision for the individual teacher, who must tap on his or her experience and professional judgement to decide what will work best for a particular class of pupils.

The cautionary notes above can be best summarised by stating that an interactive whiteboard has the potential to make a good teacher better, but at the same time it can make a poor teacher even worse and, on its own, it's never going to compensate for poor-quality teaching.

Practical considerations

The trouble with builders and those responsible for maintaining the fabric of our schools is that they rarely consult teachers before embarking on a project in schools. You will find no better example of this than the positioning of interactive whiteboards on classroom walls up and down the country, but particularly in Key Stage 1 classrooms where, typically, the pupils are barely able to reach halfway up the board. This problem is not confined to primary schools. When the rooms used for initial teacher training in my own institution were equipped with interactive whiteboards, they were positioned such that I, despite being over six feet tall, was unable to reach to the top. For my vertically challenged colleagues this was an even greater problem and so naturally we were very keen for it to be resolved. Instead of simply lowering the interactive whiteboard, the solution that the builders came up with was to construct a large raised platform in the area in front of it. Now every time I step up to use the whiteboard I don't know whether to crack a few jokes, break into song or recite from Shakespeare! Thankfully for my students I have resisted all temptation and have limited my repertoire strictly to the teaching of mathematics.

So, regardless of whether you work in Foundation Stage or in Higher Education, you need to make sure that interactive whiteboards are installed such that all potential users can reach them comfortably and safely. Essentially this is an equal opportunities issue as well as one of health and safety. Recently I was talking to the head of a local primary school that had just been equipped with an interactive whiteboard in every classroom, including the Reception class. She said that she had measured the height that every Reception pupil could reach comfortably with the preferred writing hand and then worked out the average of these reach-heights (she didn't say whether she had used the mean, median or mode so I'll leave you to decide which is the most appropriate!). The builders were instructed to position the whiteboard in the Reception class such that the average reach-height was at least three-quarters of the way up the board. Being a builder, of course, the foreman responded with a sharp intake of breath and a slow shake of the head, saying, 'I don't know about that, love; it's not going to be easy, you know', but the headteacher persevered. As a result of this careful planning and delicate negotiation, all the Reception pupils can now use the interactive whiteboard comfortably, although the teacher does have to kneel down to use it!

Another consideration when locating a new interactive whiteboard, particularly when you have only one, is in which classroom to put it. Many schools, when acquiring their first interactive whiteboard, decide to locate it in the computer suite. I think this is a big mistake because the range of ways in which it can be used here is very limited. Typically, it is used for little more than demonstrating skills during ICT lessons and so has a limited impact on the quality of teaching and learning. As we have already started to see in this chapter, an interactive whiteboard has a great deal to offer and I believe the best way of realising its potential is to locate it in a classroom, not the computer suite.

Sometimes schools are faced with a choice between an interactive whiteboard which is fixed permanently to a wall and one on a movable stand. This is a difficult decision because both options have their advantages. A mobile whiteboard means that potentially all teachers and therefore all classes of pupils can benefit from using it, but on the negative side there is the inconvenience of having to move it from room to room and set it up each time. Also remember that a mobile whiteboard requires a mobile digital projector and computer, so there are both the health and safety issues associated with cables trailing across the classroom and the problem of having to calibrate the equipment at frequent intervals because it is constantly being jarred out of position. Schools with this sort of mobile equipment are also preferred by most burglars. These disadvantages may deter already reluctant staff from taking the plunge and trying out the new technology. They see the interactive whiteboard as an inconvenient option that they are more than happy to avoid. In several schools I have seen these sorts of barrier result in mobile whiteboards not being used at all, spending most of their time locked away in a storeroom.

When an interactive whiteboard is fixed to the wall of one classroom, it is difficult for all classes to benefit from it, but as a permanent fixture it can simply mean switching on the equipment and making an immediate start. Also, because a fixed whiteboard is available all of the time the teacher is more likely to make regular use of it and therefore become more confident and familiar with it, unlike the mobile whiteboard scenario. Inevitably, one teacher and one class of pupils will benefit most, but this is probably better than diluting the impact of one mobile whiteboard throughout the school. The teacher with the whiteboard may act as a catalyst to bring about change amongst other staff as additional equipment is purchased in the medium and long term. In the short term there is the possibility of arranging some room-swapping so that other staff and classes can use the limited resources.

Health and safety considerations have already been mentioned above in relation to the height of the interactive whiteboard and the problem of trailing cables, but another important issue to be aware of is the effect of looking directly into the beam from a digital projector. This is particularly a problem when the projector is at table-top level as opposed to being ceiling-mounted. Always remind pupils never to look directly into the beam and ask them to step to one side before turning to face the rest of the class. Another problem with a projector that is not ceiling-mounted is that it is within the reach of the pupils and it will get very hot. Again, constant reminders are essential.

Stages in the use of an interactive whiteboard

As with any new piece of technology a teacher cannot be expected to use an interactive whiteboard to its full potential from the outset; you need to start with a few basics and build up gradually so that, as your confidence and expertise develop, you are able to explore and use some of the more advanced possibilities. Below I have identified four stages through which you might pass as you develop your expertise in using an interactive whiteboard. The rate at which you progress will depend on a number of factors, for example your initial levels of ICT confidence and competence, and your ease of access to an interactive whiteboard. Like all new skills it's a case of 'practice makes perfect' and so you will need to be able to put in a few hours at playtimes, lunchtimes and after school.

Stage 1: Swap the mouse for the pen

The first requirement is to have the computer, the digital projector and the interactive whiteboard connected correctly, ready for use. In most cases the equipment is a permanent feature in the room and so does not have to be set up every time it is used; it should be a case of simply switching on the three pieces of equipment, but sometimes in a particular order! If you are left to juggle with an assortment of computer cables, sockets, plugs and adaptors then you ought to seek technical advice from someone else in the school until you are sure which bit goes where.

Assuming that all is up and running, the first skill to master is calibrating the board so that the pen or stylus is synchronised with the mouse pointer. If the board is not calibrated then you will find yourself pointing at the whiteboard, but the mouse pointer will be elsewhere. The calibration procedure varies depending on the brand of whiteboard but it usually requires you to point with the pen at several dots or crosses on the board. Do it as accurately as you can, otherwise the board will be poorly calibrated. If the whiteboard and projector are fixed to the wall and ceiling (respectively, otherwise you may have a problem!) then it should be necessary to calibrate the board only once at the start of every day. If either piece of equipment is not fixed and may therefore be knocked out of position, then you will need to calibrate more frequently.

Once the equipment is calibrated, you can use the pen, stylus or, with some boards, your finger, as an alternative to the mouse. You can start programs, open and close files, click on toolbar buttons and menus, highlight cells on a spreadsheet or blocks of text in a document, all by pointing and dragging with the pen, and all without having to sit at the computer. This first, elementary stage on its own opens up a range of possibilities in terms of what you can do with the whole class, not just in mathematics but in all areas of the curriculum. For example, in a literacy lesson you could present a word-processed piece of text and then, after interacting with the pupils, highlight a particular word, phrase or sentence, by dragging with the pen, and then change the colour of that text or highlight it in a particular colour by clicking on the appropriate button on the toolbar. Some generic or 'content-free' software commonly used in primary schools, for example *TextEase* and *My World*, allows the user to drag text and pictures around the screen and so is ideally suited for use with an interactive whiteboard. There are also many examples of mathematics-related software that can be used in a similar fashion, one obvious (and free!) example being the Interactive Teaching Programs (ITPs), which are available in the mathematics section of the Primary National Strategy website. Specific examples of how you can use an interactive whiteboard in mathematics are provided later in this chapter.

The only thing you will not be able to do at this stage is enter text onto the screen, for example when naming a file that you are saving; at the moment you will have to resort to the computer keyboard. However, all interactive whiteboards offer an on-screen keyboard that you can use for this purpose, but we'll save that feature for later.

Stage 2: Get scribbling!

Once you've mastered the art of pointing and dragging with the pen, the next stage is to make use of the writing facilities that all interactive whiteboards offer. The precise way that you access these facilities varies from one brand of whiteboard to another, but it will probably involve a floating toolbar of writing tools on which you must click with the pen or stylus. With one particular whiteboard, which is widely used in primary schools, it is simply a case of picking up the appropriately coloured pen from the tray at the bottom of the board and writing on the surface. The writing tools that are commonly available are a pen, a highlighter and a rubber. In the case of the first two it is possible to select from a palette of colours and in all three cases the thickness can be altered to suit your requirements. Now that you have these sorts of facility at your disposal you can start to develop new techniques: words, phrases, sentences or objects on the whiteboard can be highlighted in a colour of your choice; existing text can be crossed out and alternatives squeezed in above or at the side; a quick annotation or working out can be jotted down to assist your interactions with the pupils; a particular side or angle of a shape can be identified clearly by adding an arrow or shading. These techniques can be used in conjunction with any software that is being used at the time, be it 'content-free' software such as a spreadsheet, word-processor or presentation tool or, alternatively, software specific to mathematics such as the ITPs mentioned in the previous section. Using these tools takes a bit of practice, particularly the handwriting aspect, but again it's a case of 'practice makes perfect'.

The only limitation with this way of working is that as soon as you want to return to using the software on which you have written, you lose the annotations. However, for a quick jotting or scribble to enhance the quality of your interactions with pupils it is more than adequate. If you want to keep what you've put on the board then you need to move on to Stage 3.

Stage 3: Using the flipchart or notebook facility

All interactive whiteboards provide a window where you can write and draw, but with the added feature of being able to switch away from it and then switch back again at any time. This facility is best thought of as a flipchart, notebook or jotter that has an unlimited number of pages that you can make use of. You can browse through these pages in order or jump to a particular page, and you can save your flipchart and open it again another time. By using this as an alternative to a traditional whiteboard and dry-wipe marker pen you can quickly refer back to notes and examples that were discussed earlier in the lesson and thus provide enhanced opportunities during the plenary or in subsequent lessons. How many times have you said to a class of pupils, 'So do you remember what we learned at the beginning of the week when we...'? The flipchart facility means that you can now *show* them what they were doing at the beginning of the week instead of having to rely on their vague recollections.

The final point to make is that your effective interactions with the class may well involve pupils coming out to the whiteboard and recording information on it. Their work, like your own, can be recalled and used during discussions at a later stage in the lesson or in subsequent lessons.

Stage 4: Tools and resources galore!

Using the writing tools and flipchart facilities is just the tip of a very large iceberg with regard to what's available with most interactive whiteboards. The precise nature of what's on offer varies from one brand to another but typically, in relation to mathematics, you will be able to:

■ Create flipcharts in advance that incorporate text, graphics, sounds, videos, animations and hyperlinks.

■ Access a variety of flipchart backgrounds such as horizontal lines, square grids, isometric grids, square-spotty patterns, triangular-spotty patterns.

- Use a palette of drawing tools to create various shapes, lines and arrows.

- Access a range of mathematics resources such as number lines, number grids (e.g. 100-squares and multiplication squares), digit cards, place value charts.

- Make use of on-screen tools such as rulers, protractors and electronic calculators.

- Enter typed text, for example when using a spreadsheet or data-handling software, by using the on-screen keyboard.

- Make use of an on-screen clock or countdown timer when the pupils are engaging in timed activities, for example during the oral-mental starter or during cooperative 'think-pair-share' activities.

- Use the camera or screen-capture facility to copy some or all of what is currently displayed on the whiteboard and paste it into your flipchart.

These sorts of facility mean that you can work in ways that have hitherto been impossible and the only limitation is your own confidence and imagination. However, remember the words of caution that were raised earlier: the quality of the learning experience for the pupils should always be the overriding priority, not the technology itself.

Examples of interactive whiteboard use in mathematics teaching

This section provides several examples of how you can start to use your interactive whiteboard in your mathematics teaching. In order to provide a comprehensive selection of suggestions for you to dip into, the stages of interactive whiteboard use identified above have been combined with the three parts of a typical daily mathematics lesson (starter, main activity and plenary) to give nine example scenarios. (Stages 3 and 4 have been combined into a single stage because the distinction between them is a relatively minor one.) The aim is not to provide a definitive list of activities that all primary teachers should be incorporating into their teaching. Instead, these examples simply illustrate that the interactive whiteboard can be used effectively in all parts of the daily maths lesson, regardless of your level of expertise. Use them to stimulate your creative tendencies and then run with some ideas of your own, not forgetting to share your experiences, ideas and resources with other staff in school.

The oral-mental starter

Stage 1

A spreadsheet, such as *Microsoft Excel*, can be used to generate random numbers and these can form the basis of whole-class activities during the oral-mental starter. For example, with a Reception or Year 1 class you might be focusing on number bonds to 10. A random number in the range 1 to 9 could be generated on the inter-active whiteboard and the pupils could use digit cards or number fans to show the appropriate number to make the number bond complete. With *Microsoft Excel* the formula for generating a number in the range A to B is:

$$=RAND()*(B-A)+A$$

and so to generate a number in the range 1 to 9 the formula would be:

$$=RAND()*8+1$$

Type this formula in cell A1 of the spreadsheet, press **ENTER** and a random number will appear. You'll quickly spot that there is a slight problem: the number generated is not an integer, but there is a solution to this. On the toolbar there should be two buttons, which increase and decrease the number of decimal places displayed in a cell. Click on the cell containing the random number formula and then click on the **Decrease Decimal** button several times until there are no decimal places being displayed. The next minor problem is the small font size: even on a large interactive whiteboard the pupils will struggle to see the numbers; you need to increase the font size so that the number takes up a considerable proportion of the screen. A bit of trial and error is needed here, but you will probably find that a size of between 100 and 150 is about right (you can use any size of your choosing, not just the ones on the drop-down list). To recalculate the random number press the **F9** key on the computer keyboard. Every time you press it, a new number is generated. But now you have another problem: you want to work at the white-board, not at the computer. Again, there is a simple solution: display a button on the toolbar that will recalculate all formulae on the spreadsheet. To do this, click on the **View** menu, then on **Toolbars**, then on **Customize**. A dialog box should appear. Click on the **Commands** tab and then on **Tools** from the **Categories** list on the left. Scroll down the **Commands** list on the right until you come to **Calculate Now**. Drag the **Calculate Now** button onto the toolbar at the top of the *Microsoft Excel* window. Now all you have to do is click on the **Calculate Now** button on the tool-bar and a new random number will be generated each time.

This might all sound rather complex but you can do all of this preparation beforehand and it should take no more than a few minutes. Remember to save the spreadsheet so that it is ready to use straight away on future occasions. You can also apply this basic principle to create other similar resources for the oral-mental starter. Figure 2.1 illustrates how two randomly generated numbers in the range 10 to 25 can be used to present quickfire questions for older pupils to answer. The formula used in this particular example is:

$$=RAND()*15+10$$

The addition and equals signs shown on the spreadsheet are simply text that is typed into the cells. You will need to experiment with the font size and the column width and it is also a good idea to centre the contents of the cells.

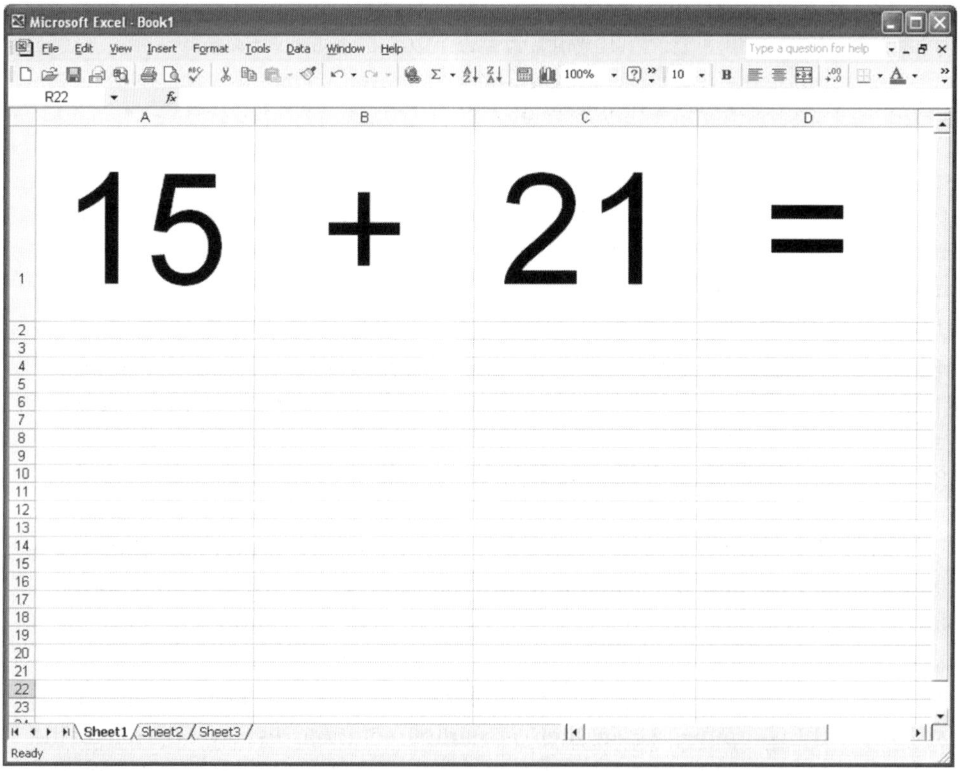

FIGURE 2.1 Using random numbers on a spreadsheet to generate questions for the oral-mental starter

Stage 2

The problem with random numbers is that they are random! I know this is stating the obvious, but the point I am making is that you have no control over what will be displayed, other than specifying the minimum and maximum values. You may therefore, by chance, generate several consecutive questions that are far too trivial for your class of pupils or at, the other extreme, produce a string of questions that are far too tricky, or even generate the same question more than once. If you are unable to live with that uncertainty then you could try an alternative approach, using presentation software such as *Microsoft PowerPoint*. Questions could be typed into the presentation, one per slide, and then displayed on the interactive whiteboard. As with the previous example, pupils could show their answers, using digit cards or number fans, to ensure that everyone participates. The advantage of this approach is that you can select the questions to meet your specific requirements. For example, you might want to include questions that become progressively more difficult, or you might want to choose numbers that emphasise a particular mental technique such as adding near-multiples of ten. At Stage 2 you should also be starting to use the interactive whiteboard's writing tools to add jottings to what is being displayed. A key feature of the oral-mental starter is that it is not just used for quickfire practice of mental skills and the recall of number facts; it should also be used to discuss and compare mental calculation strategies. So for some of the questions in the presentation you should pause to ask pupils questions such as, 'How did you get that answer?' and use jottings on the whiteboard to enhance the interaction. This is illustrated in Figure 2.2.

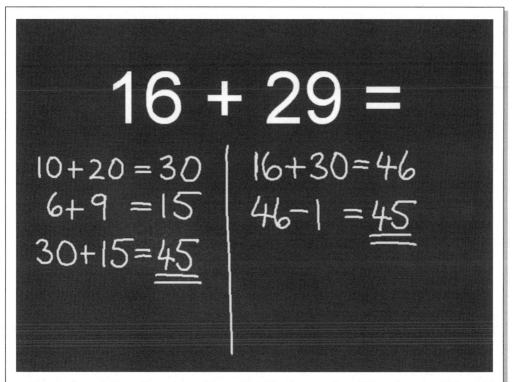

FIGURE 2.2 Presentation software to provide questions that focus on the addition of near-multiples of 10: writing tools have been used to enhance interactions with pupils

Stages 3 and 4

Once you've progressed to Stage 3 you can start to use the flipchart or notebook as an alternative to presentation software. You can also make use of a number of additional techniques that enable you to work more efficiently and also motivate your pupils. Building on the previous example you could, in advance of the lesson, use text boxes to produce a flipchart page full of questions. Each question can then be painted over with a thick pen from the palette of writing tools so that it is completely hidden from view. In the oral-mental starter all that can be seen initially on the whiteboard are the bands of colour that you used to cover the questions. Ask a pupil to pick a colour, then use the rubber tool to remove the colour and reveal a question underneath for everyone to answer. In your preparation you could use the colours randomly or perhaps as a way of addressing differentiation. Colour-code the questions according to their difficulty and then, during the lesson, say, for example, 'Now I want someone from the red group to pick one of the red questions, and remember, this one is just for the red group to answer.' Another variation is to use colour to hide just the answer to a question and then reveal the answer once pupils have attempted it themselves. This basic technique of hiding the contents of some parts of the whiteboard and then revealing them by rubbing out can be used to good effect in many aspects of the work you do, not just in mathematics. Another facility that you could use during your oral-mental starters is the on-screen countdown timer to maintain a brisk pace, as illustrated in Figure 2.3.

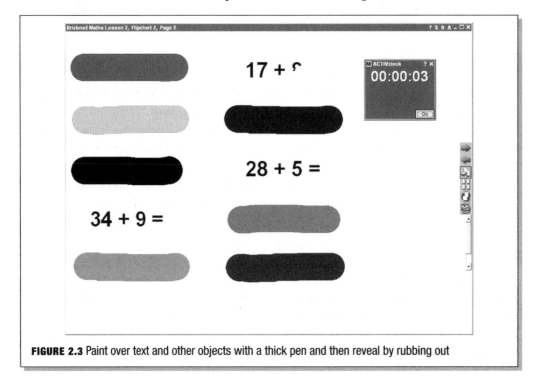

FIGURE 2.3 Paint over text and other objects with a thick pen and then reveal by rubbing out

The main activity

Stage 1

There is a huge quantity of resources, much of it freely available on the internet, that are ideally suited for use with an interactive whiteboard. Obvious examples are the Interactive Teaching Programs (ITPs), which are available from the Primary National Strategy website. Using the ITPs requires you to do nothing more than point, click and drag with the interactive whiteboard pen and so they represent an excellent first stage in the development of your skills. Spend some time familiarising yourself with what each ITP can and cannot do so that you are able to use them confidently in front of your pupils. One limitation, that will become apparent when you first start to use the ITPs, is that none of them has the facility to save your work for later use; you always have to start from scratch. However, this negative point is far outweighed by the positives:

- There are over thirty of them, covering many different aspects of mathematics.
- They are suitable for pupils throughout the primary age range.
- They can be used on a variety of computer systems (Windows-based PCs, Apple-Mac OS, etc.).
- They are very versatile and can be used in a variety of ways, unlike some electronic resources, which are very restrictive and so have only a narrow range of uses. Generally, the ITPs leave ownership of the curriculum firmly in the hands of the teachers using them rather than specify particular mathematical activities.
- They're free!

Amongst the priced software that requires nothing more than pointing, clicking and dragging with the interactive whiteboard pen are *Easiteach Maths* and *Mult-e-Maths Toolbox*. Both are designed for use with any brand of interactive whiteboard and offer a range of resources to support mathematics teaching, such as number lines, number grids, place-value charts, place-value cards, function machines, mathematical backgrounds, mathematics-related clipart. Contact details for the companies that publish these products are provided at the end of this chapter.

Stage 2

At Stage 2, as we discussed earlier in the oral-mental starter, you can start to use the writing tools to add annotations, jottings and working out to any mathematical resource that you are using with the interactive whiteboard. So, for example, if at any time you are using one of the ITPs you feel that a quick arrow, highlight or explanatory note would enhance your interactions with the pupils, then you can do this quickly and easily. Remember, though, as soon as you go back to using the ITP you will lose your annotations. If you want to keep a permanent record to use again later then you will need to progress to Stages 3 and 4.

Another example of working in this sort of way is provided by *The BFC (Big Friendly Calculator)*. This is an on-screen calculator, aimed at primary schools, that comes in two versions: a simple *Blue* version and a more elaborate *Red* version. Both are ideally suited for use with an interactive whiteboard and both have a very useful '**Calculation List**' facility which provides a permanent record of all the key presses and calculations that have been carried out. An on-screen calculator is an excellent resource to use with the whole class when looking at patterns in calculations such as those arising when multiplying by 10, 100, 1000,... A few examples could be demonstrated and discussed with the pupils, making use of the '**Calculation List**' facility to help pupils to spot the pattern in the results and to make predictions about further cases. The writing tools could be used to annotate the results and to add further explanation, as illustrated in Figure 2.4. This is an example of an appropriate use of an electronic calculator because it is not being used as a prop for simple arithmetic but, instead, as a teaching and learning tool to help pupils to spot a number pattern and understand the underlying mathematical

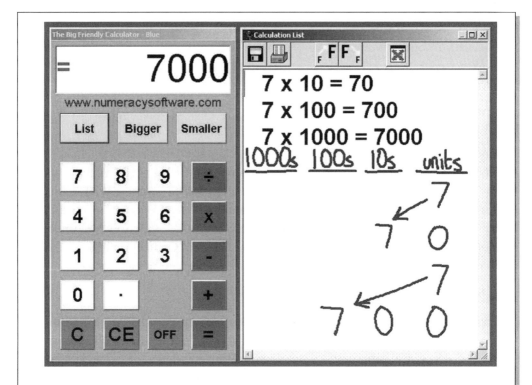

FIGURE 2.4 The *Blue* version of *The BFC*, together with annotations, to discuss patterns when multiplying by 10, 100, 1000,...

concept. Very quickly, probably after only a few minutes, the calculator will no longer be needed but it has, nevertheless, played an important role. An on-screen calculator such as this can also be used effectively when looking at mathematical areas such as:

- the relationships between fractions, decimals and percentages
- the development of 'trial and improvement' skills
- the order of precedence and use of brackets when calculating
- estimation and approximation
- the interpretation of the calculator display in problem-solving activities
- investigative activities where the focus is on higher-order thinking skills rather than on the calculations themselves
- the use of advanced features such as the memory and square root keys.

Many of these are examined in more detail in Chapter 6.

Stages 3 and 4

At Stages 3 and 4 you should first be making use of the flipchart facility to prepare simple visual aids in advance and to record the results of your interactions with pupils during the main activity. When you feel confident with this you can move on further to make use of the wealth of other resources that can be incorporated into the flipchart facility, for example, special mathematical backgrounds, number lines, number grids, digit cards, place value cards and charts, mathematical shape and line drawing tools, mathematics-related clipart, and so on. The software that comes with your interactive whiteboard may also have a 'mathematics toolbox' offering such facilities as on-screen rulers and protractors. These provide a very effective visual aid when demonstrating drawing and measuring skills to the whole class. The use of an on-screen protractor and ruler is illustrated in Figure 2.5 (page 28).

Before the advent of interactive whiteboards it was virtually impossible to demonstrate these skills effectively; it was something that usually had to be done on an individual or small-group basis. Now you have an alternative approach to call upon but there are still one or two important issues to be aware of. It is of vital importance that the experiences you share with pupils on the interactive white-board coincide with those that they have in their everyday lives. We want pupils to be able to transfer their learning from the whole-class interactive whiteboard scenario to other contexts they will encounter both in the classroom and beyond. If you've ever tried to teach pupils how to use a ruler or protractor correctly then you will be aware of the common errors they make, for example:

- They align the *end* of the ruler with the line being measured instead of aligning the *start of the scale* with the line.

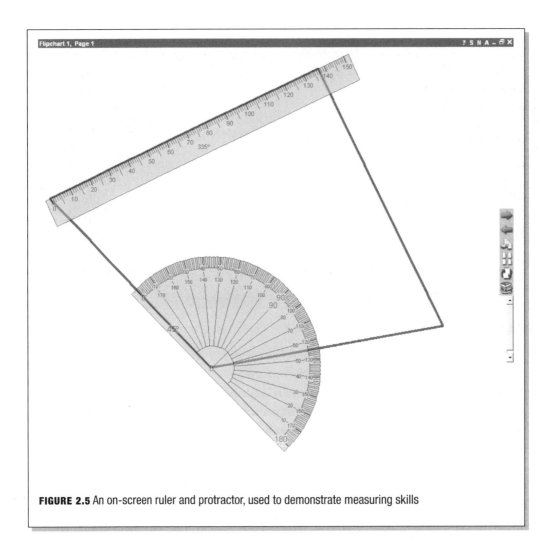

FIGURE 2.5 An on-screen ruler and protractor, used to demonstrate measuring skills

- They align the *bottom* of a semi-circular protractor with the angle instead of aligning the *horizontal baseline* of the protractor with the angle.
- They read from the *inner scale* on a protractor when they should be reading from the *outer scale*, and vice versa.

If we want pupils to be aware of and avoid these sorts of error then we need to be able to point them out when we use the interactive whiteboard. Thankfully, the ruler and protractor shown in Figure 2.5 are almost identical to the plastic rulers and protractors that most pupils in primary schools use. In this particular case you will be able to point out the pitfalls and the pupils will be able to make the link between that experience and the hands-on experiences that follow. However, some software publishers offer a simplified or sanitised version of the real world, as

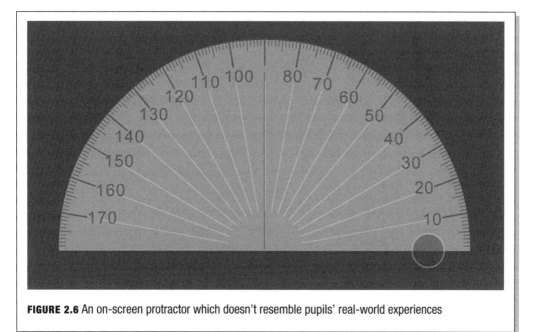

FIGURE 2.6 An on-screen protractor which doesn't resemble pupils' real-world experiences

illustrated in Figure 2.6, which shows an example of an on-screen protractor which, sadly, does not resemble those that pupils are likely to use themselves. Here the baseline of the scale coincides with the bottom edge of the protractor (rarely is this the case with a real semi-circular protractor) and there is only one scale (a real protractor usually has two). This is done with all the best intentions but it doesn't help pupils to make links in their learning and it certainly doesn't enable you to discuss potential measuring errors as effectively as you might like to. I have used this particular example to illustrate a more general point: always try to ensure that what pupils see on the interactive whiteboard reflects their real-world experiences.

The plenary

As Ofsted repeatedly reminds us, the plenary continues to be the weakest part of the daily mathematics lesson. Typically, it is used merely to provide an audience for pupils to show what they have *done* instead of what they have *learned*. The interactive whiteboard can play an important role in improving the quality of the plenary by providing a means to review and reflect upon what has been learned, to address errors and misconceptions, to use and apply the skills that have been introduced during the lesson, and to continue to assess pupil progress. An effective plenary is by no means dependent upon having an interactive whiteboard but it certainly can help, as illustrated in the following examples.

Stage 1

Part of the plenary could be set up to allow the pupils to use and apply what they have learned during the main activity but in a slightly different context. One possible context, which will surely motivate tired children at the end of a lesson, is a mathematical game. You don't have to spend too long searching on the internet to find stimulating, enjoyable activities of this sort and one particular batch of resources that you might stumble across are those on the *Primary Games* website. There are about fifty mathematics games available, covering a wide range of mathematical topics, suitable for all ages, and organised into four separate packs. These sorts of activity require nothing more than pointing, clicking and dragging with the interactive whiteboard pen and so are ideally suited to this early stage of whiteboard use.

As is always the case when selecting activities for use with pupils, you must ensure that it does what you want it to do and so is suitable in terms of content and level of difficulty. This means that you must try it out for yourself first. Don't fall into the trap of blindly picking an activity at random just to fill a few minutes during the plenary. Instead, make sure that you are choosing to use a resource for sound educational reasons that are linked to what you are trying to achieve during the lesson.

Stage 2

As we have seen previously, the next stage is to start to use the writing tools to add annotations to the interactive whiteboard. Figure 2.7 shows a *Microsoft PowerPoint* slide that was used during the plenary of a Year 6 lesson on percentages. During the main activity the pupils had been using mental skills, together with some pencil and paper jottings, to work out percentage parts. During the plenary the teacher wanted to consolidate this by getting pupils to use and apply what they had learned and also to discuss the calculating strategies they would use in different situations. At the same time the teacher also wanted to continue to assess pupil progress. As part of her preparation, the teacher, who is a confident *PowerPoint* user, created a list of percentages down the left side of the slide and a list of quantities down the right side. Each of the percentages on the left could be linked to a quantity on the right by drawing an arrow. The animation facility in *PowerPoint* can be used to make each arrow appear in turn when the mouse is clicked (or the interactive whiteboard touched). Additionally, each arrow can be made to disappear automatically when the next one appears. So, when working with the whole class during the plenary, the teacher could click on the whiteboard, resulting in a percentage being linked to a quantity with an arrow, and then discuss the question with the pupils. Another click on the whiteboard would hide the first arrow and reveal a new one. As shown in Figure 2.7, the writing tools were also used, when appropriate, to enhance the discussions.

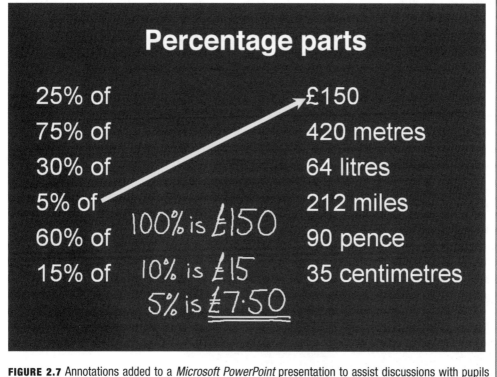

FIGURE 2.7 Annotations added to a *Microsoft PowerPoint* presentation to assist discussions with pupils during the plenary

If you're not confident enough to add animations to your *PowerPoint* presentations to make the arrows appear and disappear, don't worry; there is a simple alternative. During the plenary you could manually draw a line connecting a percentage to a quantity, discuss it with pupils, add annotations if required, and then rub it all out before drawing another line.

Stages 3 and 4

When you get to these stages, a very powerful facility, that I should strongly recommend you to investigate, is the **camera** or **screen-capture** facility. This allows you to copy some or all of what is currently displayed on the whiteboard and paste it into your flipchart. So if, whilst using any software application during the lesson, you recognise that what is on the whiteboard might be useful later, you simply take a snapshot of the screen and it will be there for you to use in the plenary.

Figure 2.8 shows a flipchart with four miniature snapshots of the ITP *Fixing Points*. The initial task in the main activity was to draw as many shapes as possible with an area of exactly 12 squares. The teacher had demonstrated and discussed a couple of examples with the pupils, using the ITP but, recognising that she would need to refer to these again later, she took a snapshot of each one and copied them into the flipchart. These are shown at the top of Figure 2.8. Later, in the main activity, the teacher wanted the pupils to find the number of dots on the perimeter and the number of dots on the inside of each shape they had drawn. She explained this by switching to the flipchart and annotating the two snapshots taken earlier. Later again in the main activity she used the ITP, together with annotations, to provide two further examples for those pupils who were still unsure. Again she took snapshots of the work, including the annotations, and copied them into the flipchart. These are shown in the lower portion of Figure 2.8. During the plenary the teacher wanted to discuss the relationship between the number of dots on the perimeter and the number of dots inside each shape. The four snapshots taken earlier proved to be invaluable in these discussions and, when information from these was combined with additional information from the pupils, the teacher was able to compile a summary of the findings, shown on the right side of Figure 2.8. By the end of the plenary many pupils were able to explain precisely the connection between the two variables.

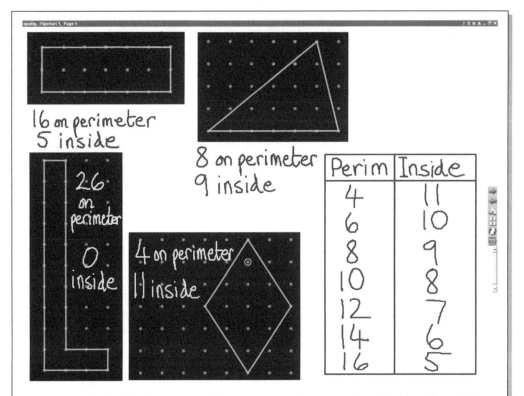

FIGURE 2.8 A flipchart for the plenary which contains snapshots taken from the interactive whiteboard earlier in the lesson

Summary

Regardless of whether you are a novice or an experienced user of an interactive whiteboard, I hope this chapter has provoked you into thinking carefully about some of the issues associated with this technology and the teaching of mathematics in primary schools. You may even have picked up a few useful tips and ideas that you can adapt for use in your own classroom. The main points that I have tried to get across in this chapter are as follows:

- The interactive whiteboard offers a huge potential in raising the quality of mathematics teaching and learning in primary schools, during all parts of the lesson, across all aspects of mathematics and with pupils of all ages.

- Teaching and learning should always take priority over the technology itself and so the *fitness for purpose* of any approach should always be a key consideration. Only use the interactive whiteboard if it offers the most effective means of achieving the learning objectives for the lesson.

- The most important interaction is that between the teacher and the pupils, not between the teacher and the interactive whiteboard. If the teacher–pupil interactions are not being enhanced then the interactive whiteboard is not being used effectively.

References and additional reading

Becta (2003) *What the Research Says about Interactive Whiteboards*. Coventry: Becta. This publication is also available at: http://www.partners.becta.org.uk/

DfEE (1999) *Framework for Teaching Mathematics from Reception to Year 6*. London: DfEE.

DfES (2004a) *Excellence and Enjoyment: Learning and Teaching in the Primary Years*. London: DfES. Details of this publication are also available at: http://www.standards.dfes.gov.uk/primary/features/learning_teaching/landt_cpd/

DfES (2004b) *ICT in Schools Survey 2004*. London: DfES. This publication is also available at: http://www.partners.becta.org.uk/

Ofsted (2003) *The National Literacy and Numeracy Strategies and the Primary Curriculum*. London: Ofsted. This publication is also available at: http://www.ofsted.gov.uk/publications/

Ofsted (2004a) *ICT in Schools: The Impact of Government Initiatives*. London: Ofsted. This publication is also available at: http://www.ofsted.gov.uk/publications/

Ofsted (2004b) *Ofsted Subject Reports 2002/03: Mathematics in Primary Schools*. London: Ofsted. This publication is also available at: http://www.ofsted.gov.uk/publications/

Ofsted (2005) *The National Literacy and Numeracy Strategies and the Primary Curriculum*. London: Ofsted. This publication is also available at: http://www.ofsted.gov.uk/publications/

Passey, D. and Rogers, C. (2004) *The Motivational Effect of ICT on Pupils*. London: DfES.

Web resources

The *Easiteach Maths* website: http://www.easiteach.com/

The *Mult-e-Maths* website: http://www.cambridge-hitachi.com/products/primary/multemaths/

The publisher of *The BFC (Big Friendly Calculator)*: http://www.numeracysoftware.com/

The *Primary Games* website: http://www.primarygames.co.uk

The *Interactive Resources* website, where you will find lots of useful mathematics resources: http://www.interactive-resources.co.uk/

The *e-chalk* website, which has resources for use with an interactive whiteboard, including a mathematics section: http://www.echalk.co.uk/

The mathematics section of the Primary National Strategy website. Here you will find the free Interactive Teaching Programs (ITPs): http://www.standards.dfes.gov.uk/primary/mathematics/

The *National Whiteboard Network* website (part of the Primary National Strategy): http://www.nwnet.org.uk/

Using one computer to support whole-class teaching

Introduction

I hope that, having read the previous chapter, you are starting to share my belief that every primary classroom should be equipped with an interactive whiteboard, but sadly this is not a reality for many teachers. Yes, there has been a massive growth in the availability of this technology in the past few years but the encouraging figure, quoted in the previous chapter, that 63 per cent of primary schools have at least one interactive whiteboard, needs to be scrutinised more critically. One obvious thing to do is to look at that figure another way: 37 per cent of primary schools do not have an interactive whiteboard. The other issue to consider is the actual number of whiteboards in a typical primary school. Amongst those schools that do have interactive whiteboards, the mean number per school is 3.1 and of these schools 60 per cent have only one or two whiteboards. The implication is that many of the teachers in the 63 per cent of schools equipped with interactive whiteboards do not actually have regular access to one. So for many teachers the only option, when it comes to using ICT in their mathematics teaching, is the solitary desktop computer that is tucked away in the corner of the classroom.

At least one computer per classroom has been a fairly typical scenario for many years now, and for some teachers this dates back to the early days of the BBC microcomputer, described in Chapter 1. However, the big problem has always been encouraging teachers actually to make use of what is available in the classroom. Getting them to switch on the computer at all is the first hurdle; ensuring they are using it effectively is the next. And I am not the only one who is saying these things. I could bore you into submission with numerous quotes from Ofsted and HMI publications from the past twenty years that support this. There are many reasons for this reluctance to embrace the technology, for example lack of confidence in using ICT, lack of staff training, lack of awareness of what is possible, and the often-quoted excuse of lack of computers. Well, yes, we should all like to have classroom access to thirty laptops for our pupils, in the same way that I should like to have access to a private jet and a chauffeur-driven limousine, but that's not the real world. I cycle to work and you have only one computer in your classroom, but we just have to live with that and make do with what is at our disposal.

The lack of awareness mentioned above refers not only to lack of knowledge of what software is available and how to use it, but also to more fundamental issues such as how to make the best use of a single computer. Most teachers think that the computer is there to be used by the pupils and yes, that is one possibility which will be considered later in this book. But one computer and thirty pupils means that each child is not going to see much of the computer in a typical week. So why not adopt an alternative approach: use the computer for whole-class teaching? By doing this you can take advantage of all the motivational aspects of ICT to capture the interest of your pupils and also use the computer to enhance your interactions with them. Yes, there will be some classroom organisational issues to consider but, with a bit of grit and determination, you will be able to overcome the potential problems and add a new dimension to your mathematics teaching.

The aim of this chapter is to provide you with some practical advice on how to use one computer effectively to support whole-class teaching. The next section looks at a range of organisational issues and how they can be overcome. Once your classroom is set up and ready, you will be poised to try one of the several example activities that are provided later in this chapter. All of them are based around a single computer, working with the whole class.

Classroom organisational issues

The location of the classroom computer reflects the way in which the teacher thinks it ought to be used. Typically, it is tucked away in a faraway, congested corner, surrounded by cupboards and tables so that the pupils using it are not a distraction to the rest of the class. However, if you want to use the computer for whole-class teaching then the first thing you need to think about is its location. Most classrooms have a carpeted area where pupils sit on the floor at various times during the day and it is here that the computer should ideally be situated. A teacher wouldn't dream of putting a blackboard, a flipchart, an easel, a 'big book' or any other visual aid where the pupils cannot see it clearly, and the same consideration should apply to the computer. Availability of electrical sockets is a restricting factor and there are also the health and safety issues associated with wires trailing across the floor but, if it is feasible, relocate the computer so that it is close to the carpeted area in the classroom. If the electrics dictate that you cannot take the computer to the carpeted area then don't give up; take the carpeted area to the computer instead! By having the computer here you will be able to gather the pupils on the floor so that they can see what is on the screen. Older children tend to be physically bigger and so get in each other's way and they also take up more space but, again, don't be put off. Move a few tables and chairs if necessary to create an 'amphitheatre' effect, with a few rows of pupils sitting on the floor close to the computer, then a row sitting on chairs and, finally, a row sitting on tables towards the back. If you are determined to use the computer then nothing should get in your way!

Another important health and safety issue, when positioning the computer, is sunlight reflecting off the screen. Pupils should not be expected to look at a computer if they have to strain their eyes. The obvious solution is to provide blinds or curtains, but if these are not available then the position of the screen will have to be adjusted. Pupils will also struggle to see small text and objects on the screen and so you need to be aware of this when you are planning computer-based activities. Ensure that the software being used is such that the pupils will be able to see what you want them to see without discomfort. I shall return to this issue later when discussing suitable software that can be used.

Assuming that you have set up your classroom computer in a suitable location, having taken account of all the necessary health and safety issues, the next thing you might like to think about is precisely where you are going to sit when you are using the computer with the class. One of the first classroom management tips that trainee teachers are offered is never to work for more than a few seconds with their backs to the class. So when working with the whole class you cannot possibly sit yourself down at the computer in the usual way. You won't be able to see the pupils and they won't be able to see the screen because you'll be in the way. Instead, you will need to sit to the side of the computer screen so that you are facing the pupils and therefore reposition the keyboard and mouse for comfortable use. The keyboard could even rest on your lap. The keyboard and mouse are likely to have wires that are at least a couple of metres long and so they can be repositioned flexibly although an alternative is to use wireless versions for complete freedom.

One final point to be aware of relates to the use of laptops or flat-panel screens. These sorts of display tend to have relatively narrow viewing angles compared to a traditional monitor. As soon as you move either left or right, away from a central viewing position, the quality reduces rapidly. A laptop, however, can be connected to an external monitor to overcome this problem.

Teaching mathematics with one computer

Many of the example activities described in the previous chapter can be adapted for use with a solitary computer as opposed to an interactive whiteboard. For example, you could present questions for the whole class during the oral-mental starter by using random numbers on a spreadsheet or through presentation software. If the numbers are made virtually to fill the screen then the pupils should have no problem seeing them clearly. Similarly the Interactive Teaching Programs (ITPs) could be used to demonstrate and discuss particular aspects of mathematics with the whole class. Obviously, you will not be able to interact with the screen as you would with an interactive whiteboard but, as was pointed out in the previous chapter, the most important interactions are those between you and your pupils. These interactions can be just as valuable when using a humble 15-inch monitor as when using a 60-inch interactive whiteboard. Ultimately, it is dependent upon the skill of the teacher, not the complexity of the technology. This also applies to the selection and use of the educational software. It is easy to be seduced by the latest feature rich packages but the key considerations should always be the quality of the mathematical content, fitness for purpose and the impact they will have on teaching and learning. For this reason I have deliberately chosen two examples of mathematical software with origins that can be traced back to the days of the BBC microcomputer. They have been updated in recent years to run on modern computers but, in terms of content and approach, they remain relatively straightforward. However, what they do, they do extremely effectively and all at minimal or zero cost, which is always a plus point!

Introducing *Counting Machine*

Counting Machine is a *Windows*-based program, very similar to *Counter*, which first appeared over twenty years ago as part of the Association of Teachers of Mathematics BBC microcomputer package called *Some Lessons In Mathematics With A Micro (SLIMWAM)*. *Counter* itself was updated a few years ago and made available on a free CD-ROM published by the DfEE as part of the *Using ICT to Support Mathematics in Primary Schools* professional development pack (DfEE 2000). *Counter* can also be downloaded from the Primary National Strategy section of the Standards Site.

As their titles suggest, these programs provide on-screen counters that can be set up to produce number sequences of varying complexity by adjusting three parameters: the first number, the first step and an amount by which the step will change with each count. For example, if you wanted to produce odd numbers, the parameters would be:

First number	1
Step	2

Similarly, if you wanted to count backwards in 5s starting at 100, the parameters would be:

First number	100
Step	−5

The final parameter enables more complex sequences to be generated, for example square numbers:

1	4	9	16	25	36	49	64	...

With this sequence, clearly the first number is 1 and the first step is 3 (from 1 to 4) but look closely to see what subsequent steps are. The second step is 5 (from 4 to 9), the third is 7 (from 9 to 16), the fourth is 9 (from 16 to 25), and so on. The step is increasing by 2 with each count. The three parameters are therefore:

First number	1
Step	3
Step changes by	2

In addition to having these three parameters at your disposal you can also change the speed at which the numbers appear on the screen and there are other features that will be described later.

Comparing *Counting Machine* and *Counter*, the key difference is the way that the numbers are displayed on the screen. *Counter* has a very eye-catching, high-tech look but the size of the numbers cannot be adjusted. At a screen resolution of 640 by 480 the numbers occupy a reasonably large proportion of the screen but at today's commonly used resolutions they are barely visible unless you are close to the computer. In contrast, *Counting Machine* lacks the high-tech look but the numbers can be adjusted to fill the screen at any resolution, making them easy to see, even from a considerable distance. Figures 3.1 and 3.2 illustrate this important difference. It is features such as this that you need to consider when evaluating and selecting software to use with the whole class.

If you are thinking that *Counting Machine* and *Counter* don't appear to do very much then you are absolutely right. The key is the teacher, who must use skill and imagination to unlock a simple piece of software to reveal a great deal of stimulating mathematics. The following examples of how *Counting Machine* or *Counter* can be used illustrate this. To avoid persistently naming both of these programs, from now on I shall refer only to *Counting Machine*, although all of the activities described can also be carried out with *Counter*.

Counting Machine in the oral-mental starter

Counting Machine is an ideal program to use with very young children, in Reception or Year 1, who are sitting on the carpet, gathered around the computer for the oral-mental starter. Set the program to count in 1s starting at 1 and then pause the counting when it gets to 3 or 4. Now start the important interaction with the pupils, by asking questions such as:

- *Who can tell me what this number is?*
- *Everyone show me that number of fingers.*
- *Would someone like to go to the number line on the wall and point at this number?*
- *Does anyone know which number comes next?*
- *What is one more than this number?*
- *What is one less than this number?*

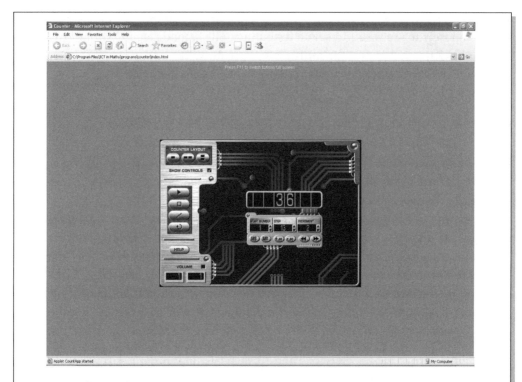

FIGURE 3.1 *Counter* used to generate square numbers. Note that the numbers occupy only a small proportion of the screen but their size cannot be adjusted

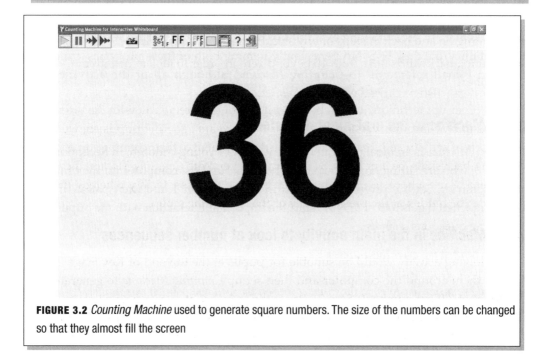

FIGURE 3.2 *Counting Machine* used to generate square numbers. The size of the numbers can be changed so that they almost fill the screen

The count can be paused and restarted at the press of a key or the click of the mouse so you can stop at any time to interact with the pupils in this sort of way. You could also use resources such as digit cards or number fans, thus allowing all pupils to give an answer to a question. Other activities that would be suitable for pupils of this age include:

- counting backwards in 1s from 10, pausing at regular intervals to interact with the pupils in the ways described above
- whole-class chanting of the numbers whilst *Counting Machine* counts, both forwards and backwards
- covering the screen with a book whilst the pupils continue to count in their heads. After a short while, pause the counting and say 'Stop!' The pupils must guess what the number is on the screen (they can use digit cards or number fans) and then you reveal the answer by removing the book.

With older pupils these sorts of oral-mental activity can be extended to include:

- counting on from zero in steps of 2 (even numbers)
- counting on from one in steps of 2 (odd numbers)
- counting on from zero in steps of 5 and 10, then later in steps of 3, 4, 6, 7, 8 and 9
- as above but counting backwards from an exact multiple, for example, backwards in 4s starting at 40
- counting on in steps of any size but not starting from zero, for example in 3s starting at 2
- counting on and back in steps of any size, from any starting number
- counting backwards in 1s from 10 beyond zero in order to look at negative numbers.

The 'cover-up' technique with a book is one that I used regularly with the original BBC microcomputer version of *Counter* many years ago. The pupils enjoyed these sorts of activity and it really helped the development of their counting-on and counting-back skills, be it in 1s, 3s, 8s, 10s or whatever. With *Counting Machine* there is no need to use a book to cover the screen because there is a facility whereby the screen can be hidden at the press of a key or the click of the mouse.

Counting Machine in the main activity to look at number sequences

The following activity would be suitable for pupils at the top end of Key Stage 2. Gather them around the computer and then set up *Counting Machine* to generate multiples of 7 (First number 0, Step 7). Pause the sequence at appropriate points and discuss it with the pupils. Then move on to a more challenging sequence, for example counting back in 6s starting at 100 (First number 100, Step –6). Again, discuss this with the pupils. Now share with the pupils the way that *Counting Machine* generates these sequences, perhaps by displaying the **Settings** box and discussing the two parameters that are required. The final stage of your interaction with the pupils should involve a number sequence that does not change by a constant amount, by making use of the third parameter. Here are some parameters you could use.

First number	1
Step	2
Step changes by	1

These will generate triangular numbers on the screen (1, 3, 6, 10, 15, 21, 28 …). Pause the counting after a few seconds and ask pupils to predict what the next number will be. Resume the counting to see if they were right and then pause it again before the next number appears. Again, ask for a prediction and also ask pupils to explain in their own words what is happening. You might want to make use of the **Number List** facility to assist your discussions of how the sequence is being generated, explaining how the first step is 2, the next step is 3, the next step is 4, and so on. This is illustrated in Figure 3.3. Then display the **Settings** box and explain the third parameter to the pupils and how it has been used to generate this particular sequence.

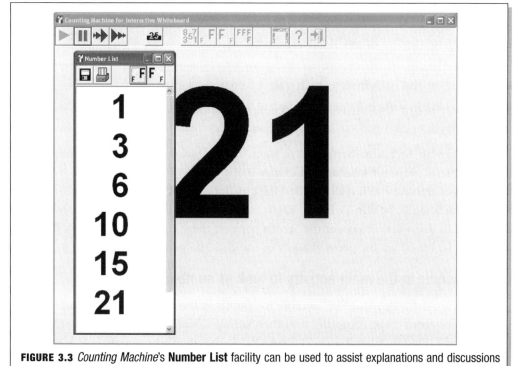

FIGURE 3.3 *Counting Machine's* **Number List** facility can be used to assist explanations and discussions with pupils

Now give the pupils a turn. You need to provide them with various number sequences and they have to work out the *Counting Machine* parameters that would be required to generate each one. You could simply write number sequences on the board or on a handout but a more creative approach is to make use of number grids such as a 100-square or a multiplication tables grid. You may already have these valuable visual aids displayed on your wall for the pupils to refer to but, if not, you could produce them as a handout. The specific tasks for the pupils could be to:

- Choose the numbers in any row, column or diagonal on the grid. This could be in any direction, for example from left to right, right to left, top to bottom, bottom to top, sloping downwards or sloping upwards.
- Write down the numbers in order and also the next three numbers in the sequence.
- Work out the *Counting Machine* parameters needed to generate the number sequence. Some sequences might need only two parameters. More complex sequences may require all three.

Because the sequences vary in difficulty there will be opportunities for you to differentiate the tasks as appropriate. For example, a row from left to right on a 100-square would involve a simple sequence such as:

21   22   23   24   25   26   27   . . .

In contrast, one possible sequence sloping upwards from left to right on a standard multiplication tables grid is:

9   16   21   24   25   24   21   16   9

Perhaps you ought to give the second one a try yourself, just to keep you on your toes and to make sure that you have been paying attention! The answers are given at the end of this chapter.

This activity provides you with an obvious focus for the plenary. Gather the pupils around the computer and ask individuals to tell the rest of the class about one of the sequences they have chosen, to discuss the next three numbers in the sequence, and finally to enter the parameters onto the computer to generate the sequence on the screen for everyone to see. As before, the Number List facility can be used to display the complete sequence to assist your discussions.

Counting Machine in the main activity for problem-solving

Problem-solving and investigative work comprise an area that is not given suffi-cient emphasis in mathematics. We have become very proficient at teaching pupils the purely mechanical skills of calculating, both mentally and using pencil and paper techniques, but this progress has not been matched in the area of using and applying these skills. Pupils are still not provided with sufficient opportunities to develop skills such as investigating, predicting, generalising, providing reasoned arguments and exploring alternative approaches, despite the fact that these have all been part of the National Curriculum since it first appeared in 1988. The following example demonstrates how *Counting Machine* can be used to promote this neglected aspect of the mathematics curriculum.

Counting Machine can display two counters on the screen simultaneously and their parameters can be set independently. Set up two counters using the following parameters:

Counter 1

First number	100
Step	−3

Counter 2

First number	0
Step	3

Start the counting and let it run for several seconds before pausing it. Ask pupils to explain in their own words what is happening, perhaps using the **Number List** facility to aid your discussions, as illustrated in Figure 3.4. Then ask pupils if they think the two counters will ever show the same number at the same time. If they think they will, then they must predict what that number will be. If they think not, then they must explain why not. Allow them a minute or two to discuss this in pairs, then discuss the problem with the whole class. Hopefully someone will be able to explain that the two counters will not show the same number at the same time, based on observations such as:

- *The bottom counter shows multiples of 3 and the top one doesn't.*
- *The two counters always add up to 50 so, in order for them to be the same we should have to see 50 on each counter and this is not possible because 50 is not a multiple of 3.*

You might be surprised by the high level of understanding that is demonstrated by the pupils' explanations and so why not provide them with more of these sorts of opportunity to articulate their thoughts?

If necessary, continue the counting to show that the two counters do not in fact show the same number at the same time. The next question to ask is:

What is the nearest number to 100 that we can start the top counter from in order to have the same number on both counters simultaneously?

Invariably, someone will suggest 99, because it is the nearest multiple of 3 to 100, so use this, even if other suggestions are offered. Start the counting and then ask pupils to predict what the simultaneously displayed number will be. At this point some pupils might spot that it is not going to happen, based on the fact that the two

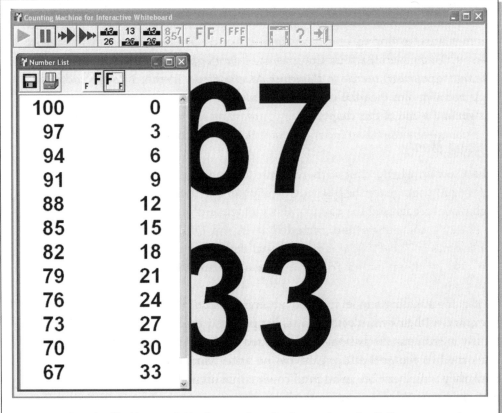

FIGURE 3.4 *Counting Machine* can display two counters simultaneously, each with its own parameters

counters now always add up to 99 and so we would have to see 49.5 on each counter, which clearly is not possible. Encourage pupils to articulate their thoughts and discuss these with the whole class.

So we know that for the top counter 100 is not suitable and 99 is not suitable. Now give the pupils a turn. Working collaboratively in pairs they must:

■ Work out the starting number nearest to 100 for the top counter which will result in the same number being displayed on both counters simultaneously.

■ Predict what the simultaneously displayed number will be.

■ Work out the other three nearest starting numbers to 100 that will also work and predict the simultaneously displayed number for each one.

In terms of mathematical content there is nothing substantial in this activity since it involves nothing more than counting on and back in 3s. But in terms of the skills that are part and parcel of the National Curriculum attainment target *Ma1 Using and Applying Mathematics*, this is a very rich and worthwhile activity.

If you want to differentiate the activity, look for ways to make it more accessible for weaker pupils; for example, they could consider the situation where the counters are counting up and down in 5, 10s or 2s. Similarly, you could ask more able pupils to generalise their findings; in other words, *What do you notice about the four starting numbers nearest to 100 which do work for us?* Perhaps you would like to keep one step ahead of the pupils and work this out for yourself? You'll find the answer at the end of this chapter.

Introducing *Monty*

Like *Counter*, *Monty* first slithered onto our computer screens as part of the *SLIMWAM* package for the BBC microcomputer over twenty years ago. Someone in high places recognised the value of this vintage offering and so updated it for use on today's computers and included it in the DfEE's *Using ICT to Support Mathematics in Primary Schools* professional development pack (DfEE 2000). *Monty* can also be downloaded from the Primary National Strategy section of the Standards Site.

The program starts by displaying a number grid of your choice. Grid 1 is a 100-square, Grid 2 is a multiplication tables grid and there are seven other grids of increasing complexity, although the first two are likely to be the most useful. After a short while the grid disappears and we meet Monty for the first time. He is a friendly python, just big enough to cover seven squares, who slithers around the grid randomly. When he stops, one of the seven numbers he is covering is revealed. The user has to try to remember what the pattern of numbers on the grid is and work out what the other six numbers are. Figure 3.5 shows Monty covering seven numbers on a multiplication tables grid (the number covered by his head has not been identified yet). If you look carefully at the way the numbers are arranged on the grid you might be puzzled by the orientation of this multiplication tables grid. The numbers are not where we might expect them to be; the multiples are increasing from right to left and from bottom to top! This is a key feature of the grids generated: they are often reflections or rotations of the conventional version we are accustomed to seeing, but this is no bad thing because it gets the pupils to think seriously about the patterns in the numbers.

Monty in the oral-mental starter

You can use *Monty* in the oral-mental starter with pupils of all ages by selecting appropriately from the nine grids that are available. Gather the pupils around the computer, select the grid you want to use and set the timer to the maximum value (200 seconds) so that you will have time to discuss the grid with the pupils before it disappears from view. With the grid displayed on the screen, interact with the pupils by asking questions such as:

FIGURE 3.5 *Monty* covering seven numbers on a multiplication tables grid – only six of them have been identified so far

- *Who knows what this number grid is?*
- *Where have you seen it before?*
- *Is it exactly the same as the one you've seen before?*
- *In what way is it different?*
- *What happens to the numbers as we move along this row?*
- *What happens to the numbers as we move down this column?*
- *The grid is going to disappear soon – do you think you can remember these number patterns?*

You can wait until the 200 seconds elapse or you can hide the grid and reveal Monty at any time by clicking on the grid. Introduce the pupils to Monty and wait for him to stop, or click on the grid to stop him at any time. Explain that Monty is covering seven of the numbers and they must work out what they are. Point to one of the squares Monty is covering and ask the pupils to tell you what the hidden number is, giving clues as necessary. To encourage everyone to participate the pupils could all give their answers by using digit cards or number fans.

Using *Monty* during the main activity

Monty is a typical example of the abundant 'drill and skill' or 'drill and practice' software that has been available to primary schools for many years. Programs such as this are primarily designed for the pupils to use but, as we have already seen above, often they offer the potential for the teacher to use them with the whole class. It is therefore important that the teacher thinks laterally and creatively about how to use a particular piece of software and not necessarily use it in the way that the publisher originally intended. Another way of being creative is to look beyond the confines of the software itself and devise for your pupils activities that are loosely related to what they have seen on the screen but that do not actually require a computer. The software is therefore used for a relatively short period of time to capture the interest of the pupils and to motivate them to tackle the subsequent activities away from the computer. So, if you have used *Monty* during the oral-mental starter you can present a *Monty*-themed task during the main activity. Several examples, suitable for all ages and abilities, are described below.

How many Montys?

You could ask pupils to investigate how many different Monty shapes there are and to record all of the possibilities on squared paper. This is not simply a case of shading seven connected squares (that activity would be 'heptominoes', very similar to the 'pentominoes' and 'hexominoes' investigations with which you may be familiar) because the seven squares must form a Monty shape that could be seen on the screen. 'Hammer-headed' (i.e. T-shaped) Montys and 'hunchbacked' Montys are not allowed! Don't be fooled into thinking that this is a mindless colouring activity; some very important mathematics is being covered here. As pupils build up their collections of Monty shapes it is likely that they will replicate one or more of them. Figure 3.6 shows three Montys that are, in fact, the same. The second one is a reflection of the first and the third one is a 180 degree rotation of the first. They are all the *same shape* but in *different positions*. So this valuable activity raises the important issue of *What do we mean by different*? Older pupils at the top of Key Stage 2 can discuss this important concept in terms of shapes being *congruent*.

Rather than this simply being a pencil and paper activity you can make it more practical by using interlocking cubes. Each pupil could be given seven cubes to construct each of their Monty shapes before recording it on paper. Remind pupils that all of the cubes must be in contact with the table because they are using the cubes to represent squares; 3-D Montys crop up later! Montys made from interlocking cubes also provide an ideal way of convincing pupils that two particular

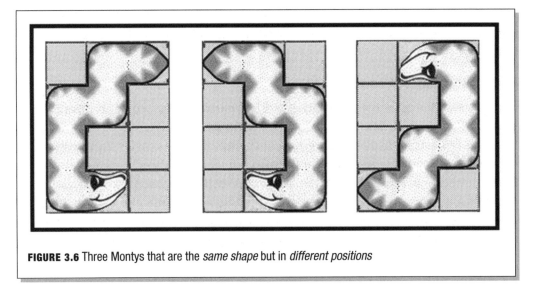

FIGURE 3.6 Three Montys that are the *same shape* but in *different positions*

examples are, in fact, the same. Simply pick one up, reflect or rotate it and then place it on top of the other. Tracing paper offers an alternative approach for addressing this particular misconception.

If you teach young children and are concerned about the complexity of working with seven squares or cubes, then you can simply adapt the activity to make it more accessible. Let them make baby Montys from four or five cubes!

Monty totals

As we have already seen, Monty covers seven numbers on a grid. Assuming this grid is a 100-square, set a target total, for example 150, and ask pupils to make a Monty and place him on a 100-square so that his total is as close as possible to the target number. Again, pupils could make their Montys out of interlocking cubes and they could create a 100-square using squared paper such that the sizes of the squares and the cubes match. During your interactions with pupils you could pose and discuss additional questions such as:

- *What happens to the total if you move Monty one square to the right?*
- *What happens to the total if you move Monty one square to the left?*
- *What happens to the total if you move Monty one square down?*
- *What happens to the total if you move Monty one square up?*
- *Can two different Monty shapes give the same total?*
- *What is the smallest Monty total you can get on a 100-square?*
- *What is the biggest Monty total you can get on a 100-square?*
- *Is it possible to make every Monty total between the smallest and the biggest?*

Not all of these questions will be suitable for all pupils but I have listed them simply to indicate the sorts of task that are possible by way of extension or follow-up.

Monty tessellations

To be honest, much of the tessellation work experienced by pupils in primary schools is pretty dull. Tessellating squares, rectangles, equilateral triangles and hexagons is usually about as interesting and challenging as it gets for the majority of pupils. With a bit of imagination and creativity on the part of the teacher it can be much more enjoyable and stimulating than this. Why not ask pupils to investigate which of the Monty shapes will tessellate? Working in pairs or small groups, they could select a particular Monty shape, use interlocking cubes to make several models of the chosen shape and then try to fit them together to construct a tessellation. Figure 3.7 shows an example of a Monty tessellation.

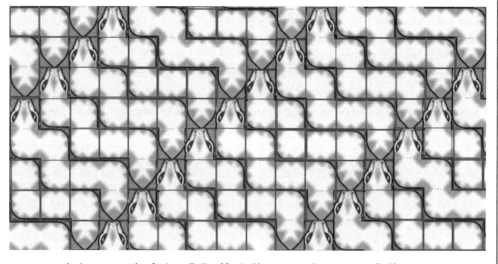

FIGURE 3.7 Just one example of a tessellating Monty. How many others can you find?

Nesting Montys

Try out this activity before setting it for the pupils. Montys are very sociable creatures and so like to huddle together with their friends.

- *Can you arrange seven Montys so that they fit snugly into a 7 by 7 square?*
- *How about a rectangular nest; for example, can you arrange ten Montys in a 10 by 7 rectangle?*

The possibilities are endless, limited only by your imagination and creativity!

Monty puzzles for your partner

We know that Monty covers seven numbers on a grid and we know that there are different sorts of grids that he slithers around on. So if we are given a Monty shape and know two of the numbers he is covering, we should be able to work out what sort of grid he is on and what the other five numbers are. Sounds easy? Well, try it for yourself, using Figure 3.8, but remember, the grids can be reflected or rotated. The answers are provided at the end of this chapter.

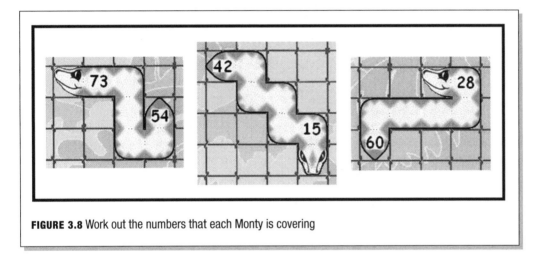

FIGURE 3.8 Work out the numbers that each Monty is covering

You could produce question sheets for your pupils in a similar fashion, but a more creative approach would be to ask pupils to make up Monty puzzles of their own to pass on to others. There is a huge potential here, not just in terms of creating and answering the puzzles, but more in terms of your discussions with pupils about the strategies they adopt when working out the missing numbers.

Monty 3-D

Monty comprises seven connected squares and he moves around on a flat 10 by 10 grid. What would he look like if he evolved into a three-dimensional Monty moving around within a three-dimensional grid? Perhaps something like the illustration in Figure 3.9.

This adds a new dimension (dreadful pun!) to the activities you can devise for your pupils and for inspiration you need look no further than those presented earlier. Pupils could make 3-D Montys out of interlocking cubes and older pupils could draw them in a 3-D style, using square-spotty or triangular-spotty paper. These sorts of 3-D drawing activity help to develop spatial awareness and are also both challenging and enjoyable.

Another possibility is to create 3-D Monty puzzles for pupils to complete, similar to the two examples shown in Figure 3.9. As with the 2-D puzzles discussed earlier, encourage pupils to devise their own, to pass on to others to complete.

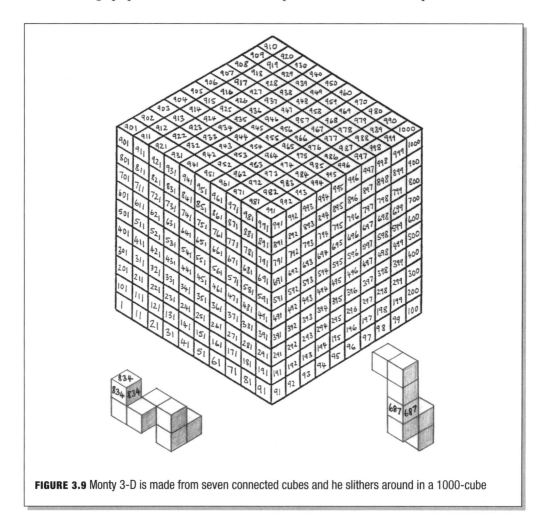

FIGURE 3.9 Monty 3-D is made from seven connected cubes and he slithers around in a 1000-cube

Summary

I hope that, having read this chapter, you are now more fully aware of the potential for using one computer to support whole-class mathematics teaching. Not all primary classrooms are equipped with an interactive whiteboard, but access to at least one desktop computer has, over the past few years, become a reality for nearly every teacher. The suggested ways of working described in this chapter therefore offer realistic possibilities for those teachers without an interactive whiteboard. Even those of you who do have access to one might like to try some of the suggested activities and approaches. However, regardless of the category into which you fall, the main points I should like you to consider are as follows.

- Be prepared to make significant alterations to the layout of your classroom in order to facilitate the use of the computer with the whole class. This might involve some initial upheaval, but it will be well worth the effort.

- Think creatively and laterally about how you can use software and web-based resources in ways other than those the publisher originally intended.

- Look at existing software and web-based resources to which you have access and evaluate them in terms of suitability for use on one computer with the whole class during the oral-mental starter.

- Evaluate software and web-based resources to see if they can be used as a starting point for related activities away from the computer during the main activity.

- Where appropriate, return to the computer during the plenary to share and discuss solutions, and to address pupils' errors and misconceptions.

Several specific examples of activities have been provided in this chapter but they are not intended to be a definitive list that you must work through. Instead, I have simply tried to illustrate, through the use of two particular pieces of software, a few of the possibilities so that you, in turn, will start to look critically at software in your own school and start to think imaginatively about how it can be incorporated into your mathematics teaching. I hope that I have demonstrated that you could probably build half a term's work around *Counting Machine* and *Monty*, and they represent just two of the thousands of computer-based resources that are available. So have a look in that box of CD-ROMs and floppy disks in the cupboard and see if there are any programs that you can start to use, no matter how old or how simple they are.

References and additional reading

DfEE (2000) *Using ICT to Support Mathematics in Primary Schools*. London: DfEE.

Details of this publication are also available at: http://www.standards.dfes.gov.uk/primary/publications/mathematics/using_ict_in_maths/

Web resources

Counting Machine is published by numeracysoftware.com: http://www.numeracysoftware.com/

Monty can be downloaded from the Standards Site: http://www.standards.dfes.gov.uk/primary/publications/mathematics/12890/

Counter is available from the Standards Site: http://www.standards.dfes.gov.uk/primary/publications/mathematics/12876/

Answers to earlier questions

Problem 1

The *Counting Machine* parameters required to generate the sequence

| 9 | 16 | 21 | 24 | 25 | 24 | 21 | 16 | 9 |

are as follows:

First number	9
Step	7
Step changes by	−2

The next three numbers in the sequence are   0   −11   −24

Problem 2

When counting up and back in 3s, the four numbers nearest to 100 that result in the counters displaying the same number simultaneously are 90, 96, 102 and 108. As you can see, these are all even multiples of 3, and they have a special name: multiples of 6!

Problem 3

The numbers in the first Monty puzzle, from head to tail, are 83, 73, 63, 64, 65, 55 and 54.

In the second puzzle they are 12, 15, 20, 24, 30, 35 and 42.

In the third puzzle they are 32, 28, 35, 40, 45, 50 and 60.

Pupils using computers in the classroom

Introduction

As was discussed at the start of the previous chapter, most teachers in primary schools have access to at least one computer in the classroom and in many cases this provision may extend to two or more. An obvious way to use this computer during mathematics lessons is to allow pupils to use it during that part of the main activity when they are working independently of the teacher, be it on their own, in pairs or in small groups. Indeed, this way of working is what most teachers understand 'using ICT' to be and so it is quite common to see the classroom computer being used in this manner. However, evidence of high-quality, effective use of the computer is less common because many teachers switch it on simply to alleviate their feelings of guilt for not using ICT as much as they ought, rather than using it for sound educational reasons to enhance pupils' learning. Many pupils are still allowed to spend time on computers in the classroom more as a reward for good behaviour or as a way of filling a few spare minutes after they have finished the 'proper' mathematics work. Identifying use of the computer as a special treat in this way is not helping in the quest to portray the computer as being just another piece of classroom equipment to be used as and when appropriate. We wouldn't reward a pupil by allowing some time playing with the overhead projector or a set of protractors so why bestow special status on the computer? The other problem with letting early finishers spend time at the computer is that these pupils are probably those who least require the additional consolidation and practice that is being offered. Often the pupils who would benefit most from a few moments at the computer are those who are struggling to complete the 'proper' work.

The aim of this chapter is to encourage teachers to facilitate the effective use of the classroom computer by pupils so that it is used for all the right reasons; that is, because it offers an effective way of achieving particular learning objectives. Important practical considerations will be considered and several mathematical approaches and activities suggested.

Key considerations

If you've already started to embrace the philosophy of the previous chapter then you will want your computer to be at the heart of the classroom, close to the carpeted area. Consequently, when a pair or small group of pupils is using the computer there might be the problem of the noise distracting the rest of the class. One possible solution is to switch off the loudspeakers, although with some software the sound effects may play a vital role in the learning experience. If this is the case then headphones offer an alternative solution. Note that it is possible for two or more pupils each to wear headphones; connect them to the same computer by using a small adapter that connects to the headphone socket.

If you have access to only a single computer then realistically no more than two or three pupils can gather around and use it effectively. If you have access to two or three computers then this allows a group of from six to nine pupils to engage in a computer-based activity, in other words, a complete ability group in a typical class.

The next important consideration is who precisely is going to use the computer in any given lesson. One concern, commonly expressed by teachers, is that with only one or two computers in the classroom it is not possible to let everyone 'have their turn'. Well, if your intention is for every pupil to spend a reasonable amount of time on every computer-based activity that you use then yes, this is a valid concern. But the question you have to ask is, 'Does every child need to do every one of the computer-based activities that I offer?' If you are using the computer for all the right reasons then the answer to this should be 'no'. You should be targeting particular pupils or groups to work on the computer because this represents the most appropriate strategy for meeting their specific needs in relation to achieving the learning objective for the current lesson. It is, therefore, not necessary for every pupil to 'have their turn' at this particular activity, although in the long term one would expect all pupils to have had an opportunity to use the computer in this way. The reasons for identifying a particular pupil or group to use the computer could be based on:

- the mathematical ability of the pupils; for example, you may target a low-ability group on some occasions and a higher-ability group on others, depending on the learning objective that has been identified and the suitability of software that is available
- the preferred learning style of particular pupils who, for some aspects of mathematics, are suited to the approach offered by a particular piece of software
- a physical disability that a particular pupil might have; for example, in some aspects of shape and space a pupil might find it difficult to draw neatly and accurately with a pencil and so a computer-based approach provides access to the curriculum

- pupil performance in the previous lesson; this may highlight the need for remedial action, in terms of an alternative approach, which can sometimes be achieved with a computer.

Another consideration is the extent to which the group using the computer will be able to make progress without the constant supervision of the teacher. This will depend on how child-friendly the particular piece of software is and so it is vital to investigate this before deciding to use it. As with any activity, computer-based or not, there are also the important issues of differentiation and matching. We don't want pupils wasting their time on trivial tasks that pose no challenge but, at the same time neither do we want them to feel completely out of their depth. One possibility to consider in this situation is the role of other adults to whom you may have access in the classroom, be it a teaching assistant, a parent or other helper. If you feel that the pupil or group of pupils would benefit from adult help then take advantage of any that is available. The benefits could be in terms of helping pupils with the practicalities of using the software or of interacting with the pupils or a combination of both. In all cases you must ensure that the other adults are briefed carefully before the lesson so that they fully understand their role and know exactly what they are expected to do.

The final issue to be considered in this section is that of assessing pupils when they are doing computer-based activities in the classroom. As with any assessment, there are two sources of evidence that will help you to make judgements in relation to the learning objectives for the lesson. First, there is the finished *product* that the pupil generates by the end of the activity, be it in an exercise book, on a worksheet or on the computer screen. You can inspect this evidence afterwards and make appropriate judgements. The problem with computer-based activities is that generally this final product is lost unless the software offers the facility for work to be saved or printed. If printing or saving is possible then you must ensure that pupils know how to accomplish this. If neither is possible then you need to check on progress at regular intervals so that you can see what is on the screen before it is lost or, alternatively, you can involve other adults as described above. Another possibility is to produce a question sheet or recording sheet to be completed by pupils whilst they are doing the activity. This helps to keep them focused on specific tasks rather than playing freely with the software.

The second possible source of evidence is the *process* that pupils go through in creating the finished product. Assessment is all about *noticing*, which is why teachers spend most of their time in the classroom observing what pupils are doing, listening to what pupils are saying, asking pupils questions and generally interacting with them. The *process* often reveals more about a pupil than does the *product*. In relation to computer-based activities the implication is that you need to observe, listen, question and interact with pupils in the same way that you would if they were working away from the computer. If, having spent twenty minutes at the computer, a group of pupils has no finished product to show you and you have not observed or interacted with them during that time, then you will be unable to make any judgements at all about the progress they have made. As indicated earlier, the computer should not be looked upon merely as a way of keeping pupils quiet for half an hour; we want them to learn something as well and we also need to know the extent to which this learning has taken place.

Examples of how to use one computer in the classroom

Before offering specific examples of activities and software that can be used I should like to identify a few general points about this way of working.

The first point relates to planning and preparation. If an individual or a small group is going to be engaged in a computer-based activity during the main part of the lesson then this must be built into your planning. You must make a conscious decision that a particular group is going to use the computer because it offers the most effective way of achieving the learning objectives. This means that at the planning stage you will need to have:

- evaluated possible software and identified something that is suitable for the age, ability and particular needs of this group
- identified specifically what you want the pupils to do at the computer
- designed, if appropriate, a question sheet or recording sheet to help to keep them focused on the specific tasks you have set
- decided whether you are going to involve another adult who will work with this group
- considered how you are going to assess pupils in this group in relation to the learning objectives for the lesson.

As can be seen from the above prompts, arranging for a group to work at the computer is not something that can be done effectively at a moment's notice. A great deal of planning and preparation is essential if you want it to be worthwhile.

Another consideration is specifically what the pupils are going to be doing at the computer in relation to everyone else. One of the underlying principles of the Numeracy Strategy is that all pupils should be engaging with the same aspect of mathematics at the same time. The days of thirty pupils all working from different pages, or indeed different books, of a mathematics scheme are, hopefully, long gone. Nowadays we should be keeping the whole class together, working on a common mathematical theme, taking account of the varying abilities of the pupils. This principle needs to be applied to any work done by groups at the computer;

that is, it should represent an alternative approach to achieving the same broad learning objectives as the rest of the class.

Software that can be used in this way

The vast majority of educational software published in the past twenty years has been written for the pupil as the end-user. It is only relatively recently, with the advent of interactive whiteboards, that publishers have started to cater for the needs of teachers who want to use software themselves to support whole-class teaching. So, with twenty years' worth of educational software out there, plus all of the web-based interactive resources that are now available, it should not be too difficult to find materials that can be used by pupils of all abilities and covering all aspects of mathematics. If anything, the problem is that there is too much available and the challenge is therefore knowing where to start. Well, why not start with what you already have in school? Have a look at the software that is installed on your computers and also dig around in cupboards to see if there are any CD-ROMs or floppy disks offering mathematical software. Spend some time exploring, investigating and evaluating such software, but always thinking about its suitability for use by your pupils to address particular learning objectives.

You could spend a small fortune on commercially available software to be used by pupils, but you don't really know what you are buying until you have actually purchased it. Some publishers offer inspection copies of their software or a free evaluation version that can be downloaded from the internet. It is better to consider these possibilities than to purchase software without the provision for returning it if it proves to be unsuitable. Another strategy is to ask colleagues in other schools what software they rate highly, perhaps with a view to visiting schools to have a look for yourself. Software evaluations can also be found on the internet, for example at the Teachers Evaluating Educational Multimedia (TEEM) website.

Often there is no need to purchase software at all because of the wealth of good-quality free resources that is available on the internet. Many schools should have a copy of the CD-ROM which is part of the *Using ICT to Support Mathematics in Primary Schools* professional development pack (DfEE 2000). This contains over ten different programs that can also be downloaded from the Primary National Strategy section of the Standards Site. Some of these are suitable for use by pupils during the main part of the daily mathematics lesson, although you do need to be aware of their limitations, as discussed below.

Three of the programs, *Carroll Diagram*, *Sorting 2D Shapes* and *Venn Diagram*, focus on the sorting of shapes. All could be used by pupils but they are very limited in their scope. Once the shapes have been sorted there is nothing else to do other than start again and repeat the activity. The shapes being sorted cannot be altered, the sorting criteria cannot be edited and there is no way of customising the program to suit pupils of varying abilities. Each program is therefore likely to occupy pupils for no more than a few minutes.

Function Machine displays a high-tech input–output machine on the screen. The user types in the input and the machine calculates the output. After repeating this several times the user must try to work out what operation or combination of operations the machine is employing. As well as being suitable for the whole class, this program offers much potential for being used by small groups of pupils at the computer. However, you would need to address differentiation by ensuring pupils select from the menu of operations appropriately and I should also recommend that you ask pupils to record their inputs and the corresponding outputs on paper, together with their answer to each problem.

Pupils can practise their angle estimation skills by using *What's My Angle*. This is a typical example of 'drill and practice' software, providing immediate feedback as soon as pupils have typed in their estimates, thus enabling them to work without adult supervision. You might want to consider the use of a recording sheet for pupils' estimates together with the true angles.

Play Train and *Toy Shop* are both suitable for use by pupils working at the computer. They focus on number and problem-solving skills, providing different levels of difficulty to assist with the differentiation. *Toy Shop* is presented as a game for two players and so there is also a strategy element.

Monty and *Counter* were introduced in the previous chapter when considering ways of using one computer to support whole-class teaching. Of the two, *Monty* is the more suitable for use by pupils because it offers immediate feedback and the different grids that are available facilitate differentiation. *Counter*, on the other hand, is largely 'content free' since it does not provide any pupil activities as such. Instead, the onus is on the teacher to devise problem-solving and investigative activities for small groups of pupils, which could be tackled using *Counter*. Such activities would need to be structured carefully and presented clearly, otherwise pupils will not know where to start and will resort to simply playing with the program. Some of the suggestions made in the previous chapter could be adapted for pupils to tackle, using *Counter*.

Another pack of five free programs worth investigating is the *Easter School CD-ROM* (DfES 2003). These programs have been designed specifically for pupils to use at the computer although you might also want to evaluate them in terms of suitability for use with the whole class. They all offer three levels of difficulty, sometimes with additional options to assist differentiation. As well as providing instant on-screen feedback, all five programs have a report facility that displays a summary of the pupils' performance, as illustrated in Figure 4.1. This can be printed out for inspection by the teacher later.

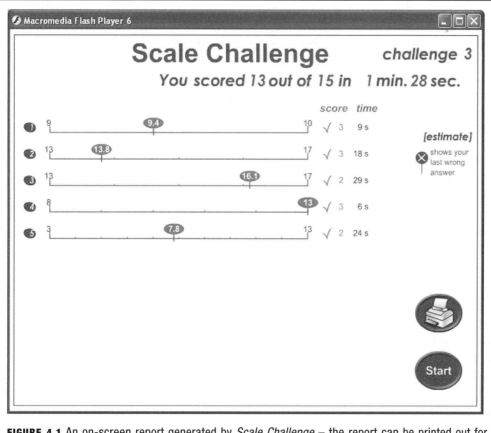

FIGURE 4.1 An on-screen report generated by *Scale Challenge* – the report can be printed out for inspection by the teacher

The five programs in the pack are:

- *Angle Challenge,* which focuses on the measuring and estimation of angles in degrees
- *Empty Box,* which provides pupils with the challenge of identifying missing digits in calculations
- *Number Strength,* which provides pupils with the opportunity to practise their mental calculation skills involving all four operations
- *Number Challenge,* which requires pupils to make a target number, using various combinations of numbers and operations
- *Scale Challenge,* which provides pupils with the opportunity to read and estimate values from scales.

The programs discussed above are not intended to form a definitive list to which you must restrict yourself. They merely represent a small fraction of what is available for pupils to use and they have the added advantage of being free. They also illustrate some of the important issues that must be considered when evaluating the suitability of software for use in this way.

Using one computer to promote collaborative group work

A common approach adopted by many teachers, right across the curriculum, is to ask pupils to work collaboratively in small groups, sharing and discussing ideas, with one person assuming the role of scribe. Most of us refer to this creative get-together as 'brainstorming' although, in a world obsessed with political correctness, this has been replaced in some quarters with the term 'thought-showers'. It is for you to decide what you want to call it, but the important point is that it is a very valuable and productive form of cooperative learning. However, it does present a number of problems. First, it is difficult for all pupils in the group to read what the scribe is writing because this is being done by hand, and for some members of the group it is upside down. Second, when the written work is submitted, there is the danger of associating the handwritten sheet more with the individual who has produced it than with the group collectively. Both of these problems may be relatively minor in the grand scheme of educating children, but there is a simple way to overcome both of them: use the computer, which is probably sitting redundant at times such as these. The scribe becomes the typist, everyone in the group can see the text clearly on the screen (increase the font size if necessary), and the printed product can be genuinely associated with the group rather than the individual who typed it. If you only have one computer then clearly only one group can work in this way on any given occasion, but in the long term you can ensure that all pupils experience this approach.

This represents yet another strategy to help ensure that the computer is used productively for as large a proportion of the day as possible and, therefore, results in more pupils being given the opportunity to use the classroom computer. The key points, as discussed earlier in this chapter, are first, to be aware of this possibility, and second, to build it into your planning and preparation for the lesson.

Data-handling with one computer in the classroom

Another way of using the class computer is to perform data-handling activities with the whole class in such a way that every pupil actually has the opportunity to use the computer, albeit for a relatively short time. Nevertheless, these sorts of activity are extremely valuable, as we shall see.

The problem with most of the data-handling experienced by pupils in primary schools is that it is dreadfully dull. Typically, the pupils are presented with a list of numbers in a textbook or on a worksheet and they are instructed to arrange the numbers in order, or to pick out all those above or below a certain value, or to draw a graph, or to work out the average. The publisher of the book or the teacher who created the worksheet pays lip-service to the notion of making the data-handling real by appending each number with 'cm' or 'kg' and informing the pupils that the numbers are, in fact, people's heights or weights. This is not real data-handling. The pupils have played no part in collecting the data, they have no ownership of the activity at all, and they almost certainly cannot see the point of all this sorting, searching, graphing and averaging. Yes, these are important skills that pupils need to develop, but surely they can be introduced in a more creative way than this? Real data-handling has to be meaningful so that the pupils can see the purpose of what they are doing, rather than doing it just for the sake of it, which has traditionally been the case.

If the data-handling is going to be real then the first step is to present to the whole class a question that needs answering, a problem that needs solving or an issue that needs investigating. For example, if you have recently been doing some work on measures with a class at the upper end of Key Stage 2, you might say to them:

- *I wonder if there is a connection between a person's height and armspan?*

Further discussion can be stimulated by asking questions such as:

- *How could we investigate this?*
- *What information do we need to gather?*
- *How are we going to collect it?*
- *What are we going to do with the data once we have collected it?*

In summary, during this first, all-important stage you need to:

- Pose and discuss a question, issue or problem with the whole class.
- Discuss what data needs to be collected.
- Discuss how the pupils are going to go about collecting the data.
- Start to discuss what will be done with the data once it has been collected.

The next stage is for the pupils to collect the data. In the case of the question posed above, this might involve them working in pairs in the classroom, measuring one another's heights and armspans and recording them on a piece of paper. Other questions could have been posed that require the pupils to do a traffic survey outside the school, or to find out what people's favourite breakfast cereals are, or to collect rainfall data from the internet for several different weather stations.

Once the pupils have data to use, the next stage is an appropriate data-handling package to record their findings on the computer. Most, if not all, schools will have access to software aimed at pupils in primary schools, for example *Pick-a-Picture, PicturePoint, RM Starting Graph, First Workshop, RM Information Magic, Information Workshop, Junior ViewPoint* and *TextEase Database*, to name just a few. With most of these packages it is not simply a case of opening the software and typing in the data. The database usually needs to be set up by the teacher first. This is likely to involve identifying how many fields (i.e. pieces of information) the database will hold, what sort of data each field will contain (text, numbers, decimals, dates, etc.), how many characters are to be allowed for each field, and you might also want to consider the use of multiple-choice options for entering the data, for example choosing from 'boy/girl' rather than pupils having to type the actual word each time.

Once you have set up the database you will need to gather the pupils around the computer and demonstrate how to enter data. In particular, show them what to do if they make a mistake. For example, if they type in 56 when it should be 65, they will need to know how to go back and change this entry. Now the pupils are ready to type their data onto the computer, and the great thing about a typical primary classroom situation is the flexibility you have in terms of organising activities throughout the day. Generally speaking, a primary teacher is with the same class all day and so the pupils can come out to the computer, one by one, throughout the day, to enter their data. Tell them to come out in register order, or give each child a number from 1 to 30, and tell them to go quietly across to the computer when they can see that it is their turn. All of this can take place whilst normal lessons are going on throughout the day. By the end of the day everyone should have entered their data onto the computer so that the complete database is ready for use the next morning.

The final stage is to gather the pupils around the computer again, this time to use the database that they have all played a part in creating. This is real data, that they have collected themselves, and, most importantly of all, they can see that it was collected for a reason. You might like to take the opportunity to use the database to revise topics that have been covered previously, for example different types of graph. You might also be able to introduce new aspects of data-handling that have not yet been introduced, for example the different types of average. However, the main focus of the discussion ought to be the original question that was posed at the first stage of the activity and how the database can be used to answer that question. In the case of the example quoted earlier (*'Is there a connection between height and armspan?'*) the discussions and demonstrations might involve:

■ making visual comparisons of the two columns containing the heights and armspans

- sorting the database according to height and then armspan. (Ask, 'Is the order very similar each time?')
- working out the difference between each pupil's height and armspan. (A spreadsheet would be an appropriate tool for this task.)
- producing a scattergraph to show the relationship between height and armspan.

I hope you agree that this sort of data-handling is far more stimulating than the typical traditional approach described earlier. My experience tells me that not only will the pupils enjoy this sort of work, they will also learn a great deal about data-handling techniques and are more likely to remember them because the experience has been real and meaningful. So why not give it a try yourself with your own pupils? To help you on your way I've described below two detailed examples of how you can put this into practice, the first aimed at Key Stage 1 and the second at Key Stage 2. A further example, suitable for Foundation Stage pupils, is discussed in Chapter 7.

An example of data-handling at Key Stage 1

Walk to School Week is a national initiative in which many primary schools partici-pate. The aim is to encourage pupils and their parents to walk to school rather than rely on other means of transport. This could be used as the stimulus for a worth-while data-handling activity with your class. During the period leading up to *Walk to School Week*, when you are explaining the initiative to pupils and distributing letters and leaflets to be passed on to parents, you could ask questions such as:

- *I wonder how many children in our class walk to school?*
- *What other ways do people come to school?*
- *How many children use these other ways of getting to school?*
- *I wonder if this is the same in other classes in the school?*

The precise questions that you pose and discuss with your pupils will depend on their age and ability and the intended scale of the activity, but the questions listed indicate the huge potential for stimulating some valuable discussion. This will need to focus on things such as:

- Who are we going to ask?
- What are we going to ask them?
- How are we going to record the information?
- Do we need to design a recording sheet?

All of this, including the possible design of a recording sheet, can be done with the whole class.

The next stage is for the pupils to go out and collect the data, in other words, conduct their survey, recording the information on the recording sheet that was designed earlier. This might be restricted to the confines of your own classroom or it might involve asking pupils in other classes, depending on decisions you made earlier about the scale and practicalities of the activity.

With regard to entering the information onto the computer you have two broad choices in terms of data-handling software. Some of the packages listed earlier are relatively straightforward and require you simply to type in the frequencies for each value so that you can then produce a graph of your choice. Others adopt a more traditional 'record card' approach whereby each person's information is entered as a separate record, which contains several fields of information. In the case of this particular example each record (i.e. pupil) might have three fields: 'Name', 'Class' and 'How I travel to school'. Again, the precise detail will depend on the decisions you made earlier during your initial discussions with the pupils.

If you adopt the first approach, then the opportunities for pupils to enter their data onto the computer are very limited but, depending on their age, ability and previous experience, this might be an appropriate choice. You will need to collate all of the information gathered by the pupils so that you have overall total frequencies for each mode of travel. There is some potential here for doing this collating and totalling whilst working with the whole class, either by working on the board or by gathering around the computer and using a spreadsheet.

If you adopt the second approach, you will have to set up the database first; that is, define each field (e.g. 'Name', 'Class' and 'How I travel to school') in terms of its name and its type (text, numbers, decimals, dates, etc.). For the 'How I travel to school' field you could use the multiple-choice options facility, if it is offered by the data-handling package you are using. The options here might include 'Car', 'Bus', 'Bicycle', 'Walk'. Once the database has been set up, you will need to demonstrate to pupils how to enter their information and then get them to try it for themselves in the flexible way described earlier in this chapter. Depending on the age and ability of the pupils, you might want to enlist another adult to assist them in this process.

With the database now complete, gather the pupils around the computer and use it to stimulate simple analysis and discussion. Here are a few areas you could explore.

Describing the data

Point to a pupil in the database and ask questions such as:

- *Which class is this person in?*
- *How does this person travel to school?*

Sorting the data

Demonstrate and explain how to sort the data alphabetically according to 'Name' and then ask questions such as:

- *What is the first name on the list?*
- *Why do you think they are first on the list?*
- *Who do you think will be last on the list?* (Then scroll down to find out.)
- *How many Peters can you see on the list?* (Repeat for other names, as appropriate.)
- *How many people have a name that begins with the letter D?* (Repeat for other letters, as appropriate.)

You could also use other fields to sort the data, for example 'Class' or 'How I travel to school', and ask other similar questions.

Graphing the data

If pupils are already familiar with different types of graph then you could use this data-handling work as an opportunity to revise what they already know. Alternatively, use it to introduce new graphs with which they are not familiar. Point to the column on the screen that lists the ways in which pupils travel to school and say:

- *Here we have this information as a list of words. How else could we show it?*

Ask pupils to describe what a particular type of graph will look like before you produce it on the screen for them to see. Once the graph is visible, ask pupils to describe and interpret it, asking questions such as:

- *Which bar is the tallest?*
- *How many people come to school by car?*
- *How many more people come by car than by bus?*

All of these discussions are just broad examples of what is possible; the precise detail of what happens in your own classroom will depend on your own particular circumstances. However, do not forget what initiated this data-handling activity in the first place; perhaps you ought to say something like:

- *What do we hope will happen during Walk to School Week?*

You could print a copy of the 'How I travel to school' graph, display it on the classroom wall and then repeat the data-handling activity during *Walk to School Week* to see if there are any changes.

An example of data-handling at Key Stage 2

Let us imagine that you have been doing a few lessons on measures with a class of pupils at the upper end of Key Stage 2 and they have experienced a range of activities involving measuring, drawing and estimating various distances. You could use this as an opportunity to do some meaningful data-handling by asking the question:

- *How could I find out how good you are at estimating distances?*

You could also introduce a comparative element by asking, for example:

- *I wonder who is better at estimating distances: boys or girls?*

or

- *I wonder if you are better at estimating distances than the other Year 5 class next door?*

Discuss this with the pupils, focusing on what information needs to be gathered and how this could be achieved. Say that you decide to identify a range of distances, ranging from just a few centimetres to several kilometres or miles, of which each pupil individually must make an estimate. Possible distances that could be used include:

- the length (in centimetres) of a small book, high up on a shelf in the classroom (out of reach so they cannot measure it!)
- the width (in centimetres) of a large poster displayed on the classroom wall
- the width or length (in metres) of the classroom
- the length (in metres) of the school hall or a particularly long corridor
- the distance (in metres) from the classroom to a distant object that the pupils can see, for example a tree on the far side of the school field
- the distance (in miles or kilometres) from the school to the city centre or to the next town or village.

Discuss with pupils how you want them to record their estimates and then give them sufficient time to complete the task. You will need to set up the database, defining a field for each estimate, plus any additional fields that are required, for example 'Gender' or 'Class', if you have included a comparative element as suggested above. Demonstrate to pupils how to enter their estimates and other information onto the computer and then set aside some time for them to build up the complete data file. One issue to bear in mind at this stage is the possibility of pupils changing their estimates as a result of seeing what others have already entered onto the computer. Many packages offer two possible ways of working when the user is entering and viewing data: Record View, in which only one record is displayed on the screen, and

List View, in which all records are displayed in tabular form, rather like a spreadsheet. Always use Record View when pupils are entering their estimates to ensure that they are not swayed at the last moment by other pupils' entries. Once complete, the data file can be used as a stimulus to revise previously covered aspects of mathematics, to introduce new ones, to focus on particular ICT skills, and to investigate the question posed at the outset. Here are a few possibilities.

Revise simple types of graph

Point to the column of information that indicates the gender of the pupils or the class they belong to and say:

- *We have shown our data as a list of words. How else could we show the data?*

Use the data to revise simple graphs such as bar charts and pie charts, remembering to ask pupils to anticipate and describe what each graph will look like before you produce it on the screen, as well as asking questions about the graphs themselves.

Introduce new types of graph

Point to one of the columns of estimates (one that includes a wide range of different numbers) and say:

- *We have shown the data as a list of numbers. How else could we show the data?*

If a pupil suggests a bar chart then follow this up by asking further questions such as:

- *What will the bar chart look like?*
- *How many bars do you think there will be?*
- *What's the minimum value in this column?* (Use the sort facility if necessary.)
- *What's the maximum value?*
- *Do you think there will be a separate bar for each value in the list?*
- *What might the label on the first bar be?*

The aim here is to introduce pupils to the concept of *grouped data,* or to revise this if it has been covered previously. Because each column of estimates probably comprises many different values, the data-handling package will organise them into categories of equal width and produce a *grouped frequency graph.* Most pupils at the upper end of Key Stage 2 need to understand the concept of grouped data and the associated graphs, and so this activity provides an ideal opportunity to do this within a real context to which pupils can relate. Produce the graph and explain the key points to the pupils. Some data-handling packages refer to this type of grouped frequency graph as a *histogram* rather than a bar chart and so you might need to discuss this contrasting terminology with pupils.

Introduce or revise the concept of average

Point to one of the columns of estimates and say to the pupils:

- *Each of you has estimated the length of the school hall but we have to choose just one value to be our class estimate. Which one should we use?*

This line of questioning and the resulting discussion will, hopefully, encourage pupils to build up an understanding of the concept of average. We have always been very good at teaching pupils the mechanical procedures for calculating the different types of average but this has not always been accompanied by sufficient emphasis on what the purpose of an average is and what it actually represents. Any average, as I am sure you already know, is a single value that typifies a set of values and it is vital that pupils appreciate this. Being able to work out the mean, median or mode is of no use at all unless you know what that number is telling you. Careful questioning and discussion, as outlined above, should enable pupils to begin to understand what averages are all about. Your discussions could focus on:

- The mean and how it is calculated. Most data-handling packages have the facility to calculate and display this.
- The median as the middle value when they are arranged in order of size. Some data-handling packages provide this but an alternative is to use the sort facility and then find the middle value in the list.
- The mode or modal group as the most popular value or most popular category if the data is grouped. This can be ascertained by looking at a graph of the data.
- The fact that the mean, median and mode are often very close to one another, because they are simply different ways of establishing what is essentially the same thing, that is, a single representative value for the set.

Answering the original question and demonstrating new ICT skills

Remind pupils of the original question that brought about this data-handling activity (*'How good are you at estimating distances?'*) and ask them how the data can be used to answer this. Hopefully, pupils will spot that at this stage the data file does not provide sufficient information to answer the question. What is needed is the error for each estimate, that is, the difference between the true distance and the pupil's value in each case. These errors could be worked out quickly but they would then need to be entered onto the computer manually, which is likely to be time-consuming since there will be several error values for each pupil. Ideally we want the computer to calculate and display these errors rather than the pupils having to do it themselves. Most data-handling packages do not offer this facility but for a spreadsheet this is a routine task, requiring the use of just a few simple formulae. This is an excellent opportunity to discuss and demonstrate how the facilities offered by traditional data-handling packages and by a spreadsheet can complement one another, and also how to carry out one or two specific ICT skills, for example:

- Saving the data in a form that can be read by a spreadsheet. Most data-handling packages offer this facility. The data is usually saved as text (*.txt*), comma separated values (*.csv*) or as an *Excel* file (*.xls*).

- Opening the file as a spreadsheet and inserting a blank first row so that headings can be typed in for each column of data. The field names are not usually retained for data saved in the way described above and so must be typed manually.

- Typing column headings for the additional information, that is, an 'Error' column corresponding to each of the distance estimate columns.

- Typing the appropriate formula in each of the 'Error' columns so that the estimate error is calculated and displayed. For example, if the poster width estimates are in column C, the poster width errors are to be displayed in column H and the true poster width is 68 cm, the following formula would be typed into cell H2:

=ABS(C2-68)

The ABS part of the formula ensures that any negative answers are displayed as positive values. We want the 'Error' column simply to display the size of the difference between the estimate and the true value; we are not interested in the direction. Please note that the availability and precise syntax of the ABS formula may vary depending on the spreadsheet you are using.

- Copying each formula down the column so that the errors for all of the distance estimates are calculated and displayed.

- Typing the appropriate formula at the bottom of each 'Error' column so that the mean error is calculated and displayed. For example, if the poster width errors are displayed in column H as far down as row 32, then the following formula would be typed into cell H34:

=AVERAGE(H2:H32)

Again, the precise syntax of this formula will depend on the spreadsheet you are using.

The techniques described above should enable you and your pupils to discuss the original question ('*How good are you at estimating distances?*') as well as any subsidiary questions such as '*Who is better at estimating distances: boys or girls?*' or '*Are you better at estimating distances than the other Year 5 class next door?*' These sorts of comparison will require additional techniques to be demonstrated and discussed, for example searching to separate the boys from the girls so that each group can be examined independently.

Other starting points for meaningful data-handling activities

The examples described above illustrate how data-handling can be made more meaningful and real than the traditional offerings to pupils, by starting with a question, a problem or an issue that needs to be investigated. However, these are based on just two of many possible starting points. Use your imagination and see what sorts of creative context you can come up with to inspire your pupils to learn how to handle data competently. Below are a few more suggestions.

Activities involving the collection of personal data, perhaps in conjunction with PE performance data, include.

- *Do boys tend to be taller, heavier and have bigger feet than girls?*
- *Are the older pupils in the class taller and heavier than the younger pupils?*
- *Do the pupils with the longest legs jump the highest and the furthest?*
- *Are boys faster runners than girls?*

Information for the analysis of weather data could be collected by the pupils themselves as part of a long-term project, downloaded from the internet or involve collaboration with schools in other parts of the country via email.

- *We've all heard about April showers but is April the wettest month of the year? Is it wetter in the spring than in the other seasons?*
- *Does our area have better weather than other parts of the country?*

The next three examples are similar to the Key Stage 2 example described in the previous section, in that they involve the comparison of two separate groups or the comparison of the same group at different moments in time.

- *Is our class better than the other class in our year group at estimating angles?*
- *Will we be better at estimating angles in one month's time (when we will have finished a block of work on shape and space) than we are now?*
- *Will our knowledge of multiplication facts improve during the coming term?*

These two examples have a language focus and could involve the comparison of texts in terms of the proportion of graphics used, the size of fonts, the number of letters per word, the number of words per sentence, and so on.

- *Are some newspapers easier to read than others? How can we tell?*
- *How can we show that Year 1 reading books are easier to read than Year 4 reading books?*

The final example is very topical, on the theme of healthy eating, and could involve pupils building up a large database of nutritional information for various foods, making use of the data displayed on food labels.

- *Which foods are good for us?*

Not all of the above examples are directly related to mathematics and so this work may occur as part of a science, a literacy, a geography or even a PE lesson, but this simply illustrates the cross-curricular nature of data-handling. However, regardless of which subject-slot on the timetable is used for this sort of data-handling, pupils will certainly be using and applying the mathematics they already know and on many occasions will be learning new mathematics as well. These sorts of cross-curricular approach are therefore fully in tune with the principles that underpin *Excellence and Enjoyment* (DfES 2004).

One final point about these sorts of data-handling activity is that they result in the creation of data files which can be stored on the school's computer network and accessed by pupils when they are working in the computer suite, assuming the school has one. Such files can be used in conjunction with carefully constructed activity sheets to provide 'hands-on' data-handling sessions. The focus could be on the development of ICT capability or mathematical knowledge, skills and understanding, or a combination of the two. Regardless of the focus, however, pupils are more likely to be inspired to learn if they are using data to which they can relate and claim ownership, than if they were to use data that holds no interest. This approach is discussed again in the next chapter.

Summary

Most primary classrooms are equipped with at least one computer and so this opens up a number of possibilities for pupils to use it during the main part of the daily mathematics lesson. If pupils are going to engage in computer-based mathematical activities then the key points to bear in mind are:

- The computer should not be used as a reward or for those who finish their other work early.
- Instead, computer-based activities should be targeted at particular pupils because this approach provides an effective means for them to achieve the learning objectives.
- If pupils are going to be doing mathematics at the computer then this must be planned for and prepared carefully in advance.

The computer can also be used to promote collaborative group work, not only in mathematics, but also in many other areas of the curriculum. Whenever small groups of pupils are sharing, discussing and recording their ideas, plan for one group to use the classroom computer. The benefits of this are that:

- All group members can see the ideas as they appear on the computer screen.
- The printed work is not handwritten and so is more likely to be associated with the group than with the individual who produced it.

Pupils can also utilise the one computer in the classroom as part of their data-handling work, not only during mathematics lessons, but also as part of a cross-curricular approach. The key points to remember are:

- Make the data-handling real and meaningful by starting with a question, problem or issue that needs to be tackled.
- Discuss this with the whole class, focusing on what data pupils need to collect and how they will do this.
- When pupils have collected the data and created a data file, use this as the basis of whole-class discussion, focusing on the revision of previously taught topics, the introduction of new concepts and skills, as well as the original question that was posed at the beginning.
- The data file created during these sorts of activity can be also be used by pupils in the computer suite to help develop their data-handling skills across the curriculum (see Chapter 5).

So with all these creative ways of using your classroom computer, there should be no excuses for it lying idle during mathematics lessons. But this is no time to be resting on your laurels; if you have access to a computer suite you can be even more creative, as discussed in the next chapter.

References and additional reading

DfEE (2000) *Using ICT to Support Mathematics in Primary Schools*. London: DfEE. Details of this publication are also available at: http://www.standards.dfes.gov.uk/primary/publications/mathematics/using_ict_in_maths/

DfES (2003) *Easter School CD-ROM*. London: DfES. Details of this publication are also available at: http://www.standards.dfes.gov.uk/primary/publications/mathematics/12816/

DfES (2004) *Excellence and Enjoyment: Learning and Teaching in the Primary Years*. London: DfES. Details of this publication are also available at: http://www.standards.dfes.gov.uk/primary/features/learning_teaching/landt_cpd/

Web resources

The TEEM website: http://www.teem.org.uk/

Pick-a-Picture, *First Workshop* and *Information Workshop* are available from BlackCat Educational Software: http://www.blackcatsoftware.com/

RM Starting Graph and *RM Information Magic* are available from Research Machines: http://www.rmplc.com

PicturePoint and *Junior ViewPoint* are available from Logotron Educational Software: http://www.logo.com/

TextEase Database is available from SoftEase: http://www.softease.com/

Teaching mathematics in the computer suite

Introduction

Until relatively recently, most primary headteachers were faced with the agonising task of deciding where to locate the scarce computer resources that their schools could afford. In broad terms, the choice was between locating all of the computers together in a computer suite or spreading them more thinly throughout the school. There are arguments in favour of both options but for most schools it was a stark choice between one or the other. In recent years, however, large injections of funding have meant that the vast majority of schools are now in the fortunate position of been able to have the best of both worlds: a computer in every classroom as well as a computer suite. This is reflected in figures published in the *ICT in Schools Survey 2004* (DfES 2004), which reveal that 77 per cent of primary schools have a computer suite and on average these comprise thirteen computers. With these facilities at their disposal, teachers can now provide computer-based lessons for whole classes of pupils, albeit typically with two pupils per computer. These could be lessons that focus on ICT capability or they could be lessons from other curriculum areas, including mathematics, which exploit the benefits offered by ICT. This opens up a whole range of possibilities in terms of creative mathematics teaching and it is the aim of this chapter to highlight some of the key issues as well as to provide a selection of example activities that you might like to try for yourself.

Key considerations

Being able to sit every pupil at a computer in the same room is essentially an extension of the scenario discussed in the previous chapter, so many of the key considerations remain unchanged and will therefore not be repeated here in detail. There are, however, a few issues that are worthy of emphasis and further discussion.

The first relates to the principle of adopting a particular approach for all the right reasons. This was considered earlier in relation to the sole classroom computer and it applies equally when access to a computer suite becomes available. Just because you are timetabled to be in the computer suite at a particular time does not mean that you have to use it just for the sake of it. It is unhelpful for classes of pupils to while away their time in the computer suite on unplanned activities that do nothing to further their learning. Instead, the teacher should be identifying specific occasions within a block of work where access to the computer suite would enhance the quality of teaching and learning, and then negotiating access at the appropriate times. It is also important that what happens in the computer suite should be fully integrated with, and complementing, the mathematics teaching in the classroom, rather than being some sort of 'bolt-on' to the curriculum. We must avoid the pitfall of thinking 'It's the third Tuesday of the month so it's time to have a maths lesson in the computer suite,' and then frantically trying to think of something to keep the pupils occupied for an hour. A computer suite is an expensive resource so, to get the best possible return on their investment, schools need to coordinate how it is going to be used across the curriculum by all age groups. This sort of planning needs to be undertaken in the medium and long term to ensure that teachers have access to the computer suite at the most appropriate times. Once the issue of access has been sorted out, it then becomes the responsibility of the individual teacher to plan and prepare in the short term, taking account of content, approach, differentiation, assessment and the role of adult support, as discussed in the previous chapter.

The second issue relates to the main focus of lessons that take place in the computer suite: specifically, the relationship between the teaching of mathematics and the development of ICT capability. In broad terms, lessons in which pupils use computers fall into one of two categories. First, there are those lessons that focus on the development of ICT capability. These are probably timetabled as 'ICT lessons' in the computer suite and the emphasis is on developing ICT skills, as outlined in the National Curriculum Programmes of Study for ICT. Second, there are lessons such as mathematics, in which pupils are using ICT because it is an appropriate tool, but the emphasis is on the mathematics rather than the ICT skills themselves. The category into which a lesson falls will be reflected in the learning objectives. In reality, however, the boundaries between these two situations are very hazy, because if pupils are using a spreadsheet to investigate number sequences during a mathematics lesson, inevitably they will be developing their ICT skills at the same time. Having said that, it is important from the point of view of both planning and assessment to decide what the main focus of the lesson is. Is it essentially a mathematics lesson or an ICT lesson? If you try to cover both at the same time, you end up with an unmanageable list of learning objectives, encompassing both mathematics and ICT, which you cannot possibly use effectively to assess pupil performance. The examples and suggestions provided in this chapter are based on the assumption that the main focus of the lesson is the mathematics and so the development of any ICT skills is incidental.

Using mathematics-specific software and web resources

In Chapter 4 it was suggested that individual or pairs of pupils could use mathematics software or web-based activities during the main part of the lesson. This principle can be extended to include all pupils in the class if a computer suite is available. All of the issues discussed in Chapter 4 will continue to be relevant for pupils working in the computer suite but, in particular, differentiation. In the classroom you only have to consider matching the computer-based activity to the ability of one or two pupils, but in the computer suite you must cater for the needs of all pupils. In terms of forward-planning and preparation, this will require you to evaluate software and web-based resources critically, ensuring that they are suitable for use by your pupils and that they offer the facility to work at different levels. Other considerations, all of which were discussed in the previous chapter, include the possible use of a recording sheet, the role of other adults and how you are going to assess pupil progress. Examples of specific computer-based resources that can be used by pupils in this way were discussed in the previous chapter and so will not be presented here.

Using the Interactive Teaching Programs

The ITPs were discussed in Chapter 2 when we were considering the use of interactive whiteboards in the teaching of mathematics. These are computer-based resources, primarily designed to be used by the teacher in conjunction with an interactive whiteboard to promote effective interaction with the whole class. There are over thirty ITPs, covering a range of mathematical topics, and they can be downloaded free of charge from the Primary National Strategy website. Despite the fact that the ITPs were designed to be used by the teacher on an interactive whiteboard, there is no reason at all why they cannot form the basis of computer-based activities for pupils in the computer suite. To illustrate this principle, four of the ITPs have been chosen and possible pupil activities are described below.

ITP *Area*

This ITP allows the user to shade squares and half-squares on a square or square-spotty grid. Four different colours of shading are available and the size of the grid can be changed. There is also an 'elastic band' facility that enables various polygons to be created on the grid. Here are some brief outlines of activities that pupils could undertake using this ITP.

- How many different shapes can be made that have an area of exactly eight squares? (Note: If one shape can be rotated or reflected so that it is the same as another shape, then they are not considered to be different.)

■ How many different-sized squares can you make with the elastic band, up to a maximum size of 5 by 5? Work out the area of each square that you make. (Hint: There are more than five different squares – they can have sloping sides!)

■ A pentomino is a shape made from five connected squares. They must be connected along a whole edge, not solely at a corner. How many different pentominoes can you make? (Note: If one pentomino can be rotated or reflected so that it fits onto another, then they are not different.)

■ How many different nets of a cube can you find? Record them by shading squares on the grid. (Note: If one net can be rotated or reflected so that it fits onto another, then they are not different.)

It would be possible for pupils to do all of the activities above using a pencil, a ruler and a sheet of paper but, as has been discussed earlier in this book, the computer-based approach offers several advantages. Pupils will be motivated by having access to the computer, they will be able to experiment with their shapes without having to rub things out and start again, and there will be particular benefits for pupils who, for whatever reason, have poor drawing skills. Having said that, you might require pupils to record some of their ideas on paper, particularly since the ITPs do not offer the option of saving or printing.

ITP *Coordinates*

This ITP provides a coordinates grid comprising one, two or four quadrants. The user can plot individual points on the grid, draw straight lines and also produce shaded polygons. The (x, y) coordinates of any location on the grid can be displayed if required. Possible pupil activities include:

■ Plotting various points on the grid, using coordinates provided by the teacher. These could be linked to work on the names and properties of 2-D shapes; for example, three vertices of a square could be provided. Pupils must plot these and work out the coordinates of the fourth vertex.

■ Drawing a shape, possibly using coordinates provided by the teacher, and then drawing its image after a reflection in one of the axes, or after a rotation of 90, 180 or 270 degrees. Pupils could also record the coordinates of the image.

ITP *Symmetry*

With this ITP a grid is displayed on the screen together with a mirror line. The user can opt to use a vertical, horizontal or sloping mirror line. A shaded shape can be created by clicking on cells on the grid and, in a similar fashion, the user can produce the image at the other side of the mirror. The ITP will reveal the correct position of the image at the click of a button. Here are two possible pupil activities.

- You provide a worksheet comprising shapes drawn on a grid and a mirror line in which each shape must be reflected. The pupils must reproduce each shape on the screen, using the ITP and then the image. The checking facility can be used to provide feedback and pupils could possibly record their images on the worksheet so that you have a record of what they have done.

- The pupils work in pairs. One pupil could produce a shape on the screen and the other has to create its image. The checking facility can be used to see if the image is correct.

ITP *Number grid*

Initially this ITP displays a standard 100-square and offers the facility to shade any cell by simply clicking on it, or shade all those cells containing a particular multiple, or all cells containing a prime number. The starting number in the top-left corner of the 100-square can be changed and the width of the grid can be adjusted, so that, for example, you could produce a grid with numbers 11 to 15 in the first row, 16 to 20 in the second, 21 to 25 in the third, and so on. Here are a few activities that pupils could try using this ITP.

- Pupils could investigate the different patterns that are produced when a particular multiple is shaded on grids of different widths. For example:
  - What sorts of pattern are produced when multiples of two are shaded on grids of width 10, 9, 8 , 7, and so on?
  - How many different patterns are there?
  - What is the connection between the width of the grid and the type of pattern produced?
  - Can pupils make predictions and general statements about the patterns that are produced?
  - This could be repeated with other multiples.
- Identify a target number, for example 30. Pupils must shade two or more connected squares (connected along an edge, not just at the corner) that have a total of 30. Pupils can adjust the width of the grid if they want to and also the starting number in the top-left corner. You could differentiate the task by setting different target numbers for pupils of different ability.
- Pupils could shade three horizontally adjacent cells, for example 4, 5 and 6, and investigate the sum of the numbers. What is the connection between the sum and the middle number? What about three vertically adjacent numbers? Is the connection between the sum and the middle number the same? What about five connected numbers arranged in the shape of a cross?

Maths activities using Logo

Pupils should encounter Logo and other related resources as part of control technology in the ICT Programmes of Study. These sorts of experience provide opportunities for pupils to develop essential life skills such as being able to give and understand precise instructions but, sadly, the potential for teaching mathematics through Logo is not exploited in many schools. Mathematics, perhaps more than any other curriculum area, provides a context for pupils to use and apply the Logo skills they have acquired and this also makes the teaching and learning of the mathematics itself more creative and enjoyable. The key issue for schools and individual teachers is to identify those aspects of mathematics that can be enhanced by using Logo and to organise the availability of resources such as the computer suite to facilitate this. Below are several examples that illustrate how Logo can be used in this way. Additional examples are discussed in Chapter 7 when considering the use of ICT in mathematics in Foundation Stage.

Pentominoes with Logo

The pentominoes activity was described briefly in the earlier section on using the ITP *Area*. If pupils have investigated and discovered all of the pentominoes in an earlier lesson, possibly using the ITP *Area* in the computer suite, or alternatively in the classroom using other resources, this could be followed by a Logo-based lesson in which they have to write a Logo procedure for each of the twelve possibilities. The basic building block for all of the pentominoes is a square and so, perhaps, pupils could start by writing a procedure to draw this shape and then use it in all of their subsequent procedures. In terms of knowledge about angles, pupils need only to write instructions for 90 degree turns and so even pupils at the lower end of Key Stage 2 should be able to access the activity.

Nets of a cube with Logo

As part of their shape and space work, pupils might spend a lesson investigating different nets of a cube, trying to find as many different layouts as possible. This theme could be reinforced in the computer suite by asking pupils to use Logo to write a procedure for each of the nets they have discovered. Rather like the pentominoes activity described above, this requires only turns of 90 degrees and so the activity should be accessible to many pupils.

Seven-pin polygons with Logo

A seven-pin polygon has corners that all lie on a hexagonal arrangement of seven dots, as shown in Figure 5.1.

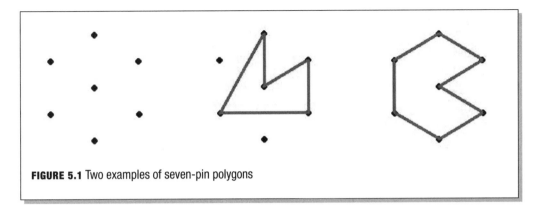

FIGURE 5.1 Two examples of seven-pin polygons

Pupils must investigate how many different seven-pin polygons they can find, perhaps using elastic bands on a pinboard, and recording their shapes on spotty paper or on a worksheet that provides blank hexagonal arrangements of dots like those shown in Figure 5.1. Rather like the pentominoes activity, this raises the important question of what we mean by *different* or, in more mathematical terms, the concept of *congruence*. It is also a valuable activity because it generates several important shapes of which primary pupils need to know the names and properties, for example equilateral triangle, isosceles triangle, right-angled triangle, rectangle, rhombus, trapezium, kite and regular hexagon. If pupils have spent a lesson in the classroom finding as many of the seven-pin polygons as they can, a follow-up lesson in the computer suite could focus on the use of Logo to write procedures for each of the shapes they have discovered. Whereas Logo commands for drawing pentominoes require only turns of 90 degrees, the seven-pin polygon procedures require a knowledge of other angles, and so this activity will be suitable for pupils at the upper end of Key Stage 2.

Tessellation with Logo

Once pupils have developed a basic understanding of tessellation through classroom activities, they could use and apply this concept in the computer suite, working with Logo. A Logo procedure could be written to produce a basic shape that will tessellate, for example a regular hexagon. This building block could then be used to create a tessellation on the screen. In doing this, pupils will have to think very carefully about moving the turtle to the correct location before drawing the next hexagon, and they will use their knowledge of angle and develop their general spatial awareness.

Symmetry with Logo

Pupils of all ages spend considerable amounts of time in the classroom looking at symmetry and related topics such as reflection and rotation, but this work is, by and large, fairly routine and predictable. A Logo-based lesson in the computer suite provides an excellent opportunity for pupils to use and apply their knowledge of symmetry in a more creative way. You could pose open-ended questions such as:

- Draw a shape with exactly one, two, three, four, ... lines of symmetry.

- Draw a shape with rotational symmetry order two, three, four, ...

- Draw a shape with rotational symmetry order two, three, four, ... but no lines of symmetry.

Older pupils can produce more elaborate symmetrical patterns by rotating a basic shape. For example, they could start by writing a procedure to produce a square:

```
TO SQUARE
REPEAT 4[FD 100 RT 90]
END
```

and then write a procedure that rotates the square to produce a symmetrical pattern:

```
TO PATTERN
REPEAT 12[SQUARE RT 30]
END
```

Pupils could experiment with the angle and the number of repeats in the **PATTERN** procedure. They could also produce patterns by rotating other basic shapes instead of a square, for example a hexagon or a circle. There is also the possibility of colouring in the resulting patterns so that they have particular symmetry properties, using either Logo itself or a drawing package such as *Microsoft Paint*.

Regular polygons with Logo

Pupils need to know the names and properties of regular polygons such as equilateral triangle, square, pentagon, hexagon and octagon. Rather than simply telling pupils about these shapes, let them be more creative in the computer suite, using Logo. In particular, this will develop an understanding of the angle properties of regular polygons and also tap on essential skills such as trial and improvement and estimation. Most pupils should encounter few problems drawing a square:

```
REPEAT 4[FD 100 RT 90]
```

and then an equilateral triangle:

```
REPEAT 3[FD 100 RT 120]
```

although many might be tempted to use 60 degrees as the amount of turn in the latter. However, the beauty of ICT is that it allows the user to experiment and refine initial ideas. In other words, if 60 degrees doesn't work, try something else instead. Pupils will get there in the end and produce a perfect equilateral triangle. In a similar fashion pupils will eventually establish the amount of turn needed to produce a regular pentagon. If their first stab is, for example, 75 degrees then the first and last sides of the pentagon will cross over one another, and so pupils have to consider what this means. Is the angle too much or not enough? Next, they might try 70 degrees and this time the first and last sides of the pentagon will not meet. Eventually, they will discover that the amount of turn is, in fact, 72 degrees and so the logo commands are:

REPEAT 5[FD 100 RT 72]

Some of the more able pupils might even spot the relationship between the number of sides (i.e. the number of repeats) and the amount of turn. If you multiply one by the other you always get 360 or, looking at it another way, the amount of turn, in degrees, is 360 divided by the number of sides.

Maths activities using a spreadsheet

Pupils are likely to be introduced to spreadsheets as part of the development of their ICT capability at the upper end of Key Stage 2 and once this has happened it opens up a range of possibilities for enhancing their mathematical experiences. The power of a spreadsheet relies on the fact that it can carry out complex calculations almost instantly, thus freeing up time for the user to concentrate on higher-level processes such as analysis, interpretation and problem-solving. The same is true of an electronic calculator (which will be considered in Chapter 6) but with a spreadsheet a large number of results can be viewed and compared simultaneously. There are many aspects of mathematics that lend themselves to the use of a spreadsheet; indeed, a whole book could be devoted to this, and so the examples described below serve only to illustrate some of the possibilities.

Investigating number sequences with a spreadsheet

A spreadsheet can be used to generate interesting number patterns such as the Fibonacci sequence:

1, 1, 2, 3, 5, 8, 13, 21, 34, 55, 89, 144, …

The sequence starts with two ones and then each subsequent number is the sum of the previous two numbers. The two ones can be typed into the first two rows of the spreadsheet and then formulae used to generate the other numbers. For example, if the two ones are typed into cells A1 and A2, the formula can be entered in cell A3 and then copied down the column as far as, say, cell A12. Once they have generated the sequence, pupils could investigate the ratio of consecutive numbers, that is, A2 divided by A1, A3 divided by A2, A4 divided by A3, and so on. This could be achieved by entering the appropriate formulae into column B of the spreadsheet. Finally, pupils could investigate what happens if the first two numbers in the sequence (the two ones) are replaced by other numbers. What effect does this have on the sequence in column A? What effect does this have on the ratios in column B? Can two numbers be used in A1 and A2 that make the twelfth number in the sequence exactly 500? There is nothing particularly special about the number 500 used in the final question; indeed, any other target number could be used. However, in tackling questions such as this, pupils will be able to employ skills such as trial and improvement, estimation and place value in the context of decimals. Perhaps you ought to try the activity yourself so that you can fully appreciate how valuable it is in relation to the development of certain mathematical knowledge, skills and understanding.

Still on the theme of number sequences, pupils could use a spreadsheet to investigate repeated halving. Suppose we started with a sheet of paper or a pizza with an area of 1000 square centimetres and then halved it. One piece is then halved again, and again, and again. If the sheet of paper or pizza is repeatedly halved ten times, what size will the final piece be? If we repeated the halving many times, what would we end up with? If all of the resulting pieces, for example half (500 cm^2) plus a quarter (250 cm^2) plus one-eighth (125 cm^2) plus one-sixteenth (62.5 cm^2), were added together, what would the total be? This problem can be investigated by means of a spreadsheet. The area of the starting piece can be entered into cell A1 and a formula can be used to carry out the repeated halving by typing into cell A2:

$$=A1 / 2$$

and copying it down the column. Each cell will then display half of what is in the cell above it. The sum of the first ten pieces can be found by using the formula:

$$=SUM(A2:A11)$$

Try it for yourself if you do not already know what the sum of all the halves will be. After that you could investigate what happens if you use repeated thirding, or repeated quartering. Can you spot a connection between the fraction you take each time and the sum of all the pieces? I won't spoil it for you – try it for yourself!

Modelling with a spreadsheet

An excellent practical investigation involving volumes of cuboids, commonly called *MAXBOX*, is described below.

- Start with a square piece of paper, for example 20 cm by 20 cm.

- Cut a small square, 1 cm by 1 cm, from each corner.
- Fold up the edges of the paper to form a shallow open-topped box.
- What is the volume of the box in cubic centimetres?
- What if you had cut a 2 cm by 2 cm square from each corner and folded up the edges of the paper? What would the volume of the box be this time?
- What if you had cut a 3 cm by 3 cm square from each corner, or a 4 cm by 4 cm square, or a 5 cm by 5 cm square, and so on?
- What is the maximum volume you can get by cutting squares like this from the corners of the paper?
- What if the squares you cut from each corner are not restricted to whole numbers? For example, you could cut a 2.8 cm by 2.8 cm square from each corner. What is the maximum volume you can get now?

Pupils could do this as a practical activity in the classroom, using a calculator for the extension stage, which involves decimal calculations, and by doing so they will be developing skills such as problem-solving, estimation and trial and improvement. As a follow-up activity in the computer suite pupils could use a spreadsheet to model this practical activity.

- Column A could be used to enter the size of the cut-out, for example 3 cm.
- Column B could contain a formula that works out the length of the box (i.e. 20 minus two lots of what is in column A).
- Column C could contain a formula that works out the width of the box (i.e. the same as the length in column B).
- Column D could contain a formula that works out the height of the box (i.e. the same as the size of the cut-out in column A).
- Column E could contain a formula that works out the volume of the box (i.e. the product of the length, width and height in columns B, C and D).

The formulae in columns B, C, D and E could be copied down through several rows of the spreadsheet and then different cut-out sizes typed into column A. By letting the spreadsheet take care of all the calculations, the pupils can concentrate fully on the problem-solving skills, the estimation skills and the trial and improvement skills. As an extension, some pupils could investigate what size cut-out gives the maximum volume when they use other starting squares. For example, what if they start with a 12 by 12 square instead of a 20 by 20? There is a connection between the cut-out that gives the maximum volume and the size of the starting square but, as before, I shall leave you to hone your spreadsheet skills by trying it for yourself!

Probability with a spreadsheet

It is important that pupils develop their understanding of probability through practical activities involving flicking coins, rolling dice, picking counters from bags, and
so on. At the upper end of Key Stage 2 they also need to appreciate the distinction
between experimental and theoretical probability. The former is obtained through
carrying out practical activities and conducting surveys. The latter is what should
happen in theory as opposed to practice. In the long run, as the number of flicks,
rolls or picks is increased, the experimental and theoretical probabilities should
become closer and closer to one another, but it is not always possible to
demonstrate this effectively in the classroom. Teachers and pupils have more
pressing things to do in mathematics lessons than flick coins or roll dice 1000 times!
This is where a spreadsheet can take over, by simulating practical probability
experiments using random numbers.

The formula:

$$= INT(RAND()*6)+1$$

will generate a random integer in the range 1 to 6 and so can be used to simulate the
rolling of a six-sided dice.

Similarly the formula:

$$= INT(RAND()*2)+1$$

generates a random number that is either 1 or 2 and so can be used to simulate the
flicking of a coin. Random numbers in the range 1 to 10 can be generated using the
formula:

$$= INT(RAND()*10)+1$$

Please note that the syntax used in these formulae is common to many spreadsheets, but you will need to check carefully for any variations. Read the instruction
manual or the help facility for your particular spreadsheet if the above formulae do
not work. You might find that there are more intuitive alternatives. For example,
Microsoft Excel offers the formula:

$$=RANDBETWEEN(a,b)$$

which generates a random integer in the range a to b.

Pupils could use formulae such as these to simulate the flicking of coins, the
rolling of dice, the picking of cards from a pack, and so on. More elaborate spreadsheets could simulate the rolling of two six-sided dice in the first two columns and
display the total dice score in a third column. Additional formulae could be used to
work out the average dice score (what would you expect it to be?) or the frequency
for each score. Just use your imagination, be creative, and try to devise spreadsheet-

based probability activities like these for your pupils. They will get a lot out of it both in terms of the mathematics and in the development of spreadsheet skills.

Data-handling activities in the computer suite

Part of Chapter 4 focused on using the classroom computer for meaningful data-handling activities with the whole class. If you adopt the approaches suggested then your pupils will create various data files that comprise real data they have collected themselves and to which they can therefore relate. Why not use these data files as the basis of follow-up activities in the computer suite? They can be stored in the shared folder of the computer network, thus enabling all users to access them easily. You could produce a carefully structured question sheet that asks pupils to investigate various aspects of the data they have collected. The key point is that the pupils have ownership of the data they are using because they played a part in the collection and this was done for a particular purpose. It is far better to use a data file of this nature than one about which the pupils know nothing.

For example, if pupils have created a data file that contain various personal measures such as height, weight, armspan, shoe size, and so on, you could pose questions such as:

- Who has the biggest armspan and what is this in centimetres?
- Produce a graph which shows all the pupils' heights. Describe the graph in your own words. Which height category is the most common?
- Investigate whether boys tend to be bigger than girls, for example taller, heavier, bigger armspans, bigger feet. Provide lots of evidence to support your answer.
- Is there a relationship between height and weight? Is there a relationship between height and armspan? Which of these two relationships is the stronger?

These four questions illustrate how you can differentiate the tasks that you set your pupils because, in terms of National Curriculum levels, they are pitched at levels 3, 4, 5 and 6 respectively. They also indicate that, by engaging in activities such as these, pupils will be developing their knowledge and understanding of data-handling from a mathematical perspective, as well as their ICT capability.

Summary

A large proportion of primary schools are equipped with a computer suite, and with careful planning this valuable resource can be used to enhance the quality of pupils' mathematical experiences and, at the same time, provide opportunities to develop ICT capability. The challenge for schools and individual teachers is to identify specific aspects of mathematics that can take advantage of a computer suite and to integrate this fully into the curriculum so that it complements and becomes a natural extension of what takes place in the classroom. This chapter has illustrated just a few of the many possibilities, covering various areas of mathematics and a range of ICT tools and resources. As is always the case with using ICT, the key to success is being prepared to dip your toe in the water and then take the plunge. Try out some of the ideas suggested in this chapter, adapting them to suit your own particular circumstances, and share your successes with other staff in your school. As your own confidence and that of your colleagues grows, you might even get to the stage where the computer suite is fully booked at those times when maths is being taught!

References and additional reading

DfES (2004) *ICT in Schools Survey 2004*. London: DfES. This publication is also available at: http://www.partners.becta.org.uk/

Web resources

The mathematics section of the Primary National Strategy website. Here you will find the free Interactive Teaching Programs (ITPs): http://www.standards.dfes.gov.uk/primary/mathematics/

If you don't have access to a Logo package then have a look at a free version called *MSW Logo*, which is available from: http://www.softronix.com/

Using calculators in mathematics

Introduction

The electronic calculator has often been portrayed as one of the major factors contributing to the decline in mathematical standards in primary schools during the 1990s. This downward spiral prompted the establishment of the government's Numeracy Task Force in 1997 and the introduction of the National Numeracy Strategy to primary schools in 1999. The publication of the final report of the task force (DfEE 1998) was accompanied by television news reports and newspaper headlines heralding the 'banning' of calculators from primary schools. This caused quite a stir in both political and education circles because it was the product of an inaccurate press release by a DfEE keen to please traditionalist commentators and the voting public. In reality, the final report recommended nothing of the sort, instead taking a more measured view on the role of calculators in primary schools:

> There is no place for using calculators as a prop for simple arithmetic...Used well, however, calculators can be an effective tool for learning about numbers and the number system, such as place value, precision, and fractions and decimals.
>
> (DfEE 1998)

Despite this measured view buried in the fine detail of the Numeracy Task Force's report, many teachers latched on to the anti-calculator hype of the headlines, ultimately causing great confusion and uncertainty as to how calculators should be used in the primary classroom. The publication of the *Framework for Teaching Mathematics* (DfEE 1999) and all the associated in-service training for teachers did little to resolve the issue, with Ofsted (2000) identifying the use of calculators as a priority area and reporting that:

> Teachers remain uncertain about when and how often to use calculators as part of their daily mathematics lessons.

Problems persisted a few years later, with Ofsted (2002) reporting that:

There is not enough good use of calculators, either as a teaching tool or by the pupils themselves, in the daily mathematics lesson.

The most recent reports from Ofsted have tended not to mention calculators and so one can only assume that no news is good news and the situation has improved.

However, one question that remains unanswered is why the calculator was afforded demonic status in the first place? The simple truth is that there is no evidence whatsoever to support the view that access to calculators has an adverse effect on pupils' ability to recall number facts and the development of their mental calculation skills. A summary of the situation is best left to the government's own School Curriculum and Assessment Authority, which, in the late 1990s, stated that:

> However tempting it may be to cast the calculator as scapegoat for disappointing mathe-
> matical performance at primary level, the available evidence provides scant support for
> this position, which may serve only to distract attention from more influential factors.
>
> (SCAA 1997)

The 'more influential factors' presumably include things such as the lack of empha-sis on mental methods and the recall of number facts, the overemphasis on traditional pencil and paper methods, the tendency to teach traditional pencil and paper methods far too early, and the overuse of individualised commercial schemes and consequent absence of any whole-class teaching. All of these were common features of primary mathematics teaching in the early and mid-1990s and, thank-fully, have all been tackled through the introduction of the National Numeracy Strategy. So do not let anybody mislead you into thinking that the advent of the calculator signalled a decline in mathematical standards in the primary school because this is simply not the case.

Now that the record has been put straight with regard to the humble electronic calculator, the rest of this chapter will be devoted to helping you make the best possible use of this valuable resource, by first ensuring that you are aware of its capabilities and then looking at specific ways in which it can enhance teaching and learning in mathematics.

Making the most of your calculator

Are you the sort of person who has a top-of-the-range microwave oven with dozens of different settings, complete with built-in grill and convection facility, but you only ever use it to heat up ready meals? Probably not, but there is an interesting parallel here with the way that most people use a calculator. Even the most basic models that are typically found in primary schools offer a range of useful features which most teachers don't even know exist and, as a consequence of this, their pupils do not find out about them either. The aim of this section is to ensure that you are fully aware of what a calculator has to offer so that you, in turn, can pass this on to your pupils at appropriate stages.

The C and CE keys

Some calculators are equipped with both a C and a CE key. The former clears a calculation completely; the latter clears only the last entry. This is particularly useful if you are adding a lengthy list of numbers but enter one of them incorrectly. Press the C key and you have to start again from scratch. Press the CE key and only the last entry will be cleared, enabling you to enter the correct number and continue with the calculation. Some calculators have only a C key which can be pressed once to clear the last entry or pressed twice to clear the complete calculation. Another variation is to have a C key to clear the last entry and a CA or AC key to clear all. Awareness of this facility can save you (and your pupils) a lot of wasted time!

Precedence of operations

Carry out the following key presses on your calculator and make a note of the answer.

Try to get hold of other makes and models of calculator, repeat the calculation and again make a note of the answers. Do you get the same answer each time or do you get different answers? The possibilities are 50 and 26. The first is obtained by simply working from left to right, carrying out each calculation in turn. The second is the result of doing the two multiplications first and then adding the two answers together. Strictly speaking the second answer, 26, is the correct one because, by mathematical convention, multiplication and division take precedence over addition and subtraction. Clearly, not all calculators are conversant with the niceties of mathematical convention, but that in itself is not something to be unduly concerned about. The important implication for you as a teacher is that first, you must investigate how the calculators used by your pupils deal with this sort of scenario, and second, you discuss the implications with them. In some respects you can turn this inconsistency between calculators to your advantage by demonstrating to your pupils the different ways that calculators operate, and then introducing the concept of brackets as a way of avoiding any potential ambiguity when writing down calculations.

Dealing with negative numbers

The results of calculations are sometimes less than zero and so a negative symbol will be displayed, but there is some variation in the way that different calculators deal with this. Commonly, the negative symbol is immediately in front of the number but occasionally it appears after the number, and sometimes the symbol is at the leftmost edge of the display, some considerable distance from the number. It is also important that you and your pupils are aware of how to enter a negative number into the display, using the +/− key, for example, when dealing with problems involving a starting bank balance which is less than zero.

Dealing with big numbers

Try working out the answer to this calculation on your calculator and see what you get in the display.

$$145\,000 \times 18\,000$$

You may get an error message because the calculator simply cannot display answers as big as this. Alternatively, you might see something like this:

$$2.61 \quad 09$$

This is an abbreviated version of *standard form* or *scientific notation* and, in full, reads as:

$$2.61 \times 10^9$$

which can be written as:

$$2.61 \times 1\,000\,000\,000$$

which is:

$$2\,610\,000\,000$$

I'm not suggesting that pupils in primary schools should be taught how to write numbers in standard form, but it is important that you know how to interpret results such as this. If able pupils in Year 6 stumble upon standard form in calculator displays you might like to try to explain it to them. The other issue to consider is alternative ways of working out $145\,000 \times 18\,000$ if the calculator cannot cope with the answer.

The constant function

Carry out the following key presses on your calculator and watch what happens.

This counting facility is an extremely powerful tool that can be used with young children, as will be discussed later in this chapter. However, it is something of which many primary teachers are completely unaware.

As well as counting on in any step, the constant function can be used to count back in any step and from any starting number, for example:

$$\boxed{6}\ \boxed{0}\ \boxed{-}\ \boxed{3}\ \boxed{=}\ \boxed{=}\ \boxed{=}$$

Multiplication and division can be used to carry out repeated doubling and halving, for example:

$$\boxed{2}\ \boxed{\times}\ \boxed{=}\ \boxed{=}\ \boxed{=}\ \boxed{=}\ \boxed{=}$$

The memory facility

Do you ever use the memory keys on your calculator? Probably not. Why? Because nobody has ever shown you how to use them. Now that is a real shame because they can save you a lot of time and effort, scribbling down intermediate answers when you are carrying out complex or lengthy calculations. Once you have mastered the memory facility yourself, make sure you teach your pupils how to use it so that they can also reap the benefits. It is a powerful feature, it is there to be used, so why not use it?

The memory facility usually comprises four keys, as described below.

M+ When you press this key, whatever is in the display is added to the memory.
M− When you press this key, whatever is in the display is subtracted from the memory.
MR When you press this key, the number in the memory is displayed.
CM When you press this key, the memory is cleared.

By using these keys you can tackle complex calculations such as:

$$(19 \times 23) + (685 \div 25) - (17 \times 12.5)$$

more efficiently by adding or subtracting the intermediate answers to or from the memory, instead of writing them down on paper.

The creative use of calculators in mathematics

Earlier in this chapter a quotation from the final report of the Numeracy Task Force was provided (DfEE 1998) which indicated some of the ways in which calculators can be used effectively in mathematics. I should like to build on that modest list of suggestions and provide a more comprehensive indication of how calculators can be used with pupils of all ages in the primary school.

Number recognition

Suggesting that calculators should be banned from primary schools, or even from Key Stage 1 classrooms, is ridiculous. How can you possibly stop young children having access to something that is part of their everyday lives, that they will use extensively throughout their schooling, and that can be found in every household up and down the country? Instead of contemplating a ban on calculators, teachers in Key Stage 1 should be actively seeking ways of incorporating this valuable resource into their teaching. This area of weakness has been noted by Ofsted (2000), which stated that:

> There is considerable confusion as to how calculators can be used as a teaching aid with younger pupils.

One area in which calculators can be used to good effect with young children is number recognition. Electronic displays are all around us and so, from an early age, children are likely to encounter them about the home in a range of household appliances. We should be bringing this alternative electronic notation to the attention of children instead of trying to present them with a sanitised version of the real world. Flashcards and wall displays could be used to discuss the ways that numbers are displayed electronically. A giant, poster-sized calculator could be a permanent visual aid in the classroom, complete with removable cardboard keys and electronic digits. These could form the basis of whole-class or small-group teacher-led activities in which the keys and electronic digits are stuck in the appropriate locations on the giant calculator, after consulting the pocket-sized versions that the pupils have in front of them. The familiar way of writing digits shown on the keys could be compared with the electronic notation in the calculator display. Sticking the keys onto the giant calculator also provides an opportunity to develop important vocabulary associated with position. For example, you could ask questions such as:

- *Which key is next to the 7?*
- *Which key is above . . . , below . . . , between . . . , to the right of . . . , to the left of . . . ?*

Another possibility is to discuss the way that the calculator actually displays the digits, using terminology such as 'light-sticks'. The digit 8 is displayed when all seven light-sticks are switched on by the calculator, whereas the digit 1 requires only two light-sticks. Discuss this electronic wizardry with the pupils and ask them questions such as:

- *How many light-sticks does number 3 use?*
- *Which digits use exactly four light-sticks?*

A more open-ended approach would be to ask pupils to find as many numbers as they can that use exactly six light-sticks. (These could be one-, two- or three-digit numbers – there are quite a few of them!) You could also ask pupils to arrange their numbers in order of size.

I hope these examples illustrate that a calculator is not something to be feared or something from which we have to protect children. Yes, it is important that the calculator should not be used as a substitute for simple mental skills, but that is certainly not the case here. Clearly, with a creative approach, the calculator can be used to very good effect.

Counting, comparing and ordering numbers

The constant function was discussed earlier in this chapter and so is now something with which you should be familiar. If you have access to a large on-screen calculator, perhaps in conjunction with an interactive whiteboard, you could use this facility as the basis of counting activities with the whole class or small groups of pupils. Counting on in 1s, you could stop after each press of the equals key and ask pupils to predict the next number. You could ask them what the number would be after three, or four, or five more presses. You could also count backwards in 1s, or forwards or backwards in any other amount, to encourage mental addition and subtraction skills.

Another possibility is to give each pupil a calculator and play *Fast-fingers*. This activity is best conducted with pupils sitting at their tables rather than on the carpet. Ensure that they all know how to use the constant function to count on in 1s and then tell them to press the 1 key, followed by the add key and to then fold their arms. Tell them that when you say '*go*' they must press the equals key as many times as they can until you say '*stop*'. Then they must fold their arms again. Try this, but do not give them too much time or they may generate very large numbers. Five seconds should be about right although you can alter this depending on the sorts of number you want the pupils to work with. After you have said '*stop*', ask various questions about what the pupils have in their displays, for example:

■ *Who has a number bigger than 30? ... less than 15? ... between 20 and 25? ... more than 35 but less than 40?'*

and so on. When pupils put their hands up, ask one or two of them what their number is, just to make sure it is right. Pick up on any errors and misconceptions by asking further questions. Your whole-class interactions could be followed by similar small-group activities. For example, a group could play *Fast-fingers*, but this time each pupil writes the number on a slip of paper and then they all have to arrange the numbers in order of size and record them in their books.

Exploring the number system

The counting-on activities, using an on-screen calculator as described above could be extended to consider big numbers and the notion of infinity. You could ask pupils what they think the biggest number is, or what number they will eventually see in the display if they keep pressing the equals key.

The same setup could be used to discuss negative numbers. You could start by counting back in 1s from, say, 10. When you pause at zero, ask the pupils what they think will come next. They may come up with some interesting suggestions. Some might think that the numbers will start to increase, whilst others may suggest that the display will stick at zero. Even if you are considering negative numbers for the first time, it is likely that there will be some pupils who are already aware of the concept and will be able correctly to tell you that the next number will be –1. The calculator is only one of a range of resources that can be used to teach negative numbers but it does have an important role to play.

Place value

An on-screen calculator, in conjunction with an interactive whiteboard, can be used to reinforce various aspects of place value. For example, when examining the effects of multiplying by 10, 100, 1000, and so on, a calculator can be used to bring the pattern to the attention of pupils. Very quickly, pupils will spot what is happening and so should be able to predict further examples without needing the calculator. In this situation the calculator has been used to help the pupils identify patterns in calculations but it can be discarded at an early stage and replaced by mental skills. The calculator has not been used as a prop for simple arithmetic but, instead, has been a valuable tool to assist the pupils' mathematical understanding.

Another example of how a calculator can be used to support place-value work is the activity *Zap the digit*. Using an on-screen calculator, enter a large number into the display, for example 3478. Tell the pupils that you want to 'zap' the 7 and replace it with a zero, but this has to be done by subtracting a number. Ask the pupils what number must be subtracted to achieve this and then use the calculator to try out the suggestions. Similarly, you could ask what has to be subtracted in order to 'zap' the 4. A few minutes spent on *Zap the digit* is time well spent because it adds another strategy to your armoury for attempting to make pupils understand what each digit in a number actually represents.

Investigating the properties of number

Numbers possess many interesting properties. They can be odd or even, prime or composite (i.e. non-prime), negative or positive, integers or fractions, or be divisible by a particular number. Knowing these sorts of property is, in itself, of little direct relevance to our everyday lives but exploring some of these properties provides pupils with excellent opportunities to develop a range of problem-solving skills that will serve them well in their general mathematical development.

Once pupils understand what a prime number is you could ask them to use a calculator to check if a given number is prime, or ask them to find all of the prime numbers between 50 and 100 or between 100 and 200. As stated above, knowing lists of prime numbers can hardly be described as a key skill but, in finding these numbers, pupils will be employing a range of problem-solving strategies that can be discussed and shared with the whole class. For example, many pupils will quickly spot that if the given number is even then it cannot possibly be prime (unless it is 2, which is the first prime number and the only prime that is even). An activity such as this could also lead to a discussion of tests for divisibility or provide a context in which this knowledge could be applied, if it has already been taught. In their search for prime numbers some pupils might realise that in the case of an odd number, such as 137, there is no point in trying to divide it by 12, or 14, or 16 or any other even number, because all multiples of these are even. These sorts of observation and discovery demonstrate higher-level thinking skills and provide excellent opportunities for discussion.

As well as classifying whole numbers as odd or even and as prime or composite, the Ancient Greeks also classified them as *defective, excessive* or *perfect*. A defective number is one that is less than the sum of its factors (not including itself as a factor). For example, the factors of 12 (excluding itself) are 1, 2, 3, 4 and 6 and the sum of these factors is 16. An excessive number is greater than the sum of its factors; for example, the factors of 14 are 1, 2 and 7, which have a sum of only 10. A number which is the same as the sum of its factors is perfect; for example, the number 6 is perfect. As part of their work on factors, pupils might like to classify numbers as defective, excessive or perfect, using a calculator where appropriate. The first four perfect numbers are 6, 28, 496 and 8128. You might like to check this for yourself by finding the sum of all their factors. If you have plenty of time on your hands you could also do this for the fifth perfect number, 33 550 336.

Numbers can also be palindromic; that is, read the same forwards as backwards, as is the case with the number 57 275. You could ask pupils to use a calculator to find palindromes with particular properties, for example:

- a palindrome greater than 100 that is also a multiple of 7
- a palindrome that is a square number
- a palindrome greater than 100 that is prime
- a palindrome that is a multiple of 12
- two palindromes with a difference of 2
- two palindromes that multiply to give a palindrome.

Again, it is the problem-solving and the associated discussion of pupils' strategies that are the most important aspect of this activity, not the fact that 999 and 1001 are two palindromes with a difference of 2.

Using the calculator as a checking tool

Throughout Key Stage 2 it is appropriate for pupils to use a calculator to check their answers to calculations that have been carried out by mental or pencil and paper methods. Obviously, this has to be monitored carefully to ensure that the calculators are not being used as a substitute for the pupils' own non-calculator methods and you will probably have to lay down ground rules for how the calculators should be used. However, once established, this approach provides pupils with a degree of independence and it also reduces the amount of work that you have to mark in detail yourself.

Using the calculator for lengthy or complex calculations

Whenever pupils are faced with a calculation, they should always consider mental methods as a first resort. If this approach is not possible, then the second consideration should be a pencil and paper method, either a traditional one or an informal alternative with which the pupil feels comfortable. Eventually, however, a point is reached where the list of numbers is so lengthy, or the numbers or calculations are so complex, that it is wholly appropriate to use a calculator. Pupils at the upper end of Key Stage 2 are likely to encounter this scenario when considering aspects of mathematics such as:

- complex calculations involving whole numbers, particularly multiplication and division, or division where a precise decimal answer is required
- complex calculations involving decimals
- problem-solving involving money (percentage increases and decreases, currency conversions, value for money calculations, etc.)
- problem-solving involving measures (distances, area, volume, capacity, metric to imperial conversions, etc.)
- calculation of mean values in data-handling activities.

If we want pupils to use a calculator effectively in such situations it is important that we address a number of key issues. First, there is the issue of pupils actually being able to use all of the calculator functions efficiently. How to make the most of a calculator was considered earlier in this chapter and it is of vital importance that this knowledge should be shared with pupils. You will, therefore, need to devise lessons that focus specifically on calculator skills so that pupils will be able to use and apply these, as a matter of course, in mathematics as well as in their everyday lives. The second key issue is that of never blindly accepting the answer in the calculator display. Pupils must be encouraged to estimate a rough answer before reaching for the calculator, so that they can look at the display and decide whether or not it looks reasonable. This requires both approximation skills (to round the numbers involved) and estimation skills (a quick mental calculation using the rounded numbers) and so these, in turn, will have to be given emphasis at appropriate points in your teaching. Another key issue is that of being able to interpret the answer provided by the calculator in the context of the problem being tackled, particularly where money is involved or where numbers must be rounded up or down, depending on the context. For example, consider these two problems:

- Seven people go out for a meal and the bill is £93. They share the cost equally. How much does each person pay?
- Seven people win £93 in The National Lottery. They share the money equally. How much does each person get?

In both cases the calculation required is:

$$93 \div 7$$

and the answer provided by the calculator is:

$$13.285714$$

but the answers to the original questions are different. Each person will pay £13.29 for the meal (There will be 3p left over which can be the tip – they are students!) and will receive a £13.28 lottery prize. (There will be 4p left over.) Being able to identify the important information and select the correct arithmetical operation is only part of the problem-solving process. You also need to interpret the answer appropriately, depending on the context, and this is of particular relevance when using a calculator.

Developing approximation skills

The importance of being able to round numbers was mentioned in the previous section. Pupils need to employ rounding skills in order to make rough estimates, and they also need to be able to round calculator answers appropriately and correctly. Pupils require rounding skills and calculators provide a resource to help practise and develop those very same skills. So if you want to provide pupils with activities that focus on rounding, why not make use of the calculator? You could provide a list of numbers from which pupils randomly select any two, and then use a calculator to divide one by the other. They must write down the precise answer and also round the answer to the nearest whole number or to one, two or three decimal places. You will have to give some careful thought to the numbers you provide on the list, otherwise the division may not result in an answer with lots of decimal places. A good choice is prime numbers (but not 2). I shall leave you to work out why.

The relationship between fractions and decimals

At the upper end of Key Stage 2 pupils need to know the decimal equivalents of common fractions and vice versa. When first discussing the relationship between fractions and decimals, the link between fractions and division, and how actually to get from three-quarters to 0.75, you might like to use an on-screen calculator to assist your interactions with pupils. Many pupils will eventually be able to recite equivalent fraction and decimal forms almost instantly but, for more complex fractions, it would be appropriate for them to use a calculator. One specific way in which this approach could be used is in ordering a set of fractions by first converting them to decimals. Pupils could also use a calculator for problem-solving and investigational work involving fractions. For example, you could ask pupils to use a calculator to work out the decimal equivalents for one-ninth and two-ninths. Then ask them to predict what three-ninths, four-ninths, five-ninths, and so on are, before checking with the calculator. Similarly you could use 7ths, 11ths, 27ths, 33rds and 37ths. In every case there is a clear pattern in the digits, which we hope pupils will spot, and then use to make predictions. Knowing that two-elevenths is 0.181 818 and three-elevenths is 0.272 727 is not, in itself, important, but identifying patterns and making predictions is.

Understanding the relationships between operations

In order to calculate efficiently, pupils need to understand the relationships between the four operations, for example the inverse relationship between addition and subtraction, and between multiplication and division. There is also the fact that multiplication can be considered as repeated addition and division as repeated subtraction. Understanding these sorts of relationship lies at the heart of effective arithmetic and so they must be taught explicitly and reinforced whenever the opportunity arises. Calculator activities such as *Broken keys* provide a way of achieving this. Pupils are required to carry out various calculations, using a calculator but with the restriction of certain keys not being available to use. Here are a few examples of the sorts of question you could pose.

- Work out $48 \div 17$ without using the division key.
- Work out 9.38×2.57 without using the multiplication key.
- Work out 3.25×18.6 without using the multiplication key.
- Work out $2500 \div 32$ without using the number 3 key.

In the first question, an understanding of the inverse relationship between multiplication and division, together with estimation skills and trial and improvement skills, can be used to find the answer. In effect, the pupils must find the number that, when multiplied by 17, gives the answer 48. Similar knowledge, skills and understanding can be employed in the second question. Here the pupils must find the number that, when divided by 2.57, gives the answer 9.38 or, alternatively, find the number that, when divided by 9.38, gives 2.57. The third question can be tackled in exactly the same way, although there is another possibility. If pupils understand that multiplication is repeated addition they can think of 3.25 lots of 18.6 as being 3 lots of 18.6 plus 0.25 lots of 18.6. The 3 lots can be obtained by repeated addition and the 0.25 lots (i.e. one-quarter) by dividing by 4. This particular question would also serve to illustrate how the memory facility can be put to good effect. Once the 3 lots have been calculated, the answer can be stored in the memory. Later, the 0.25 lots can be added to the memory and the final answer recalled. The final question can be tackled using repeated halving.

In these sorts of activity the aim is not for pupils to practise their calculating skills; that is being taken care of by the calculator. Instead, the aim is to develop an understanding of the relationships between the four operations and to reinforce estimation skills and trial and improvement methods. This will be reflected in the learning objectives that you identify for the lesson.

Developing trial and improvement skills

As has just been stated above, the *Broken keys* activities provide valuable opportunities for pupils to develop and practise their trial and improvement skills. Here are a few more examples of the sorts of question you could pose.

- A square has an area of 60 cm². Find the length of its sides without using the square root key.
- A cube has a volume of 100 cm³. Find the length of its sides.
- Two numbers have a sum of 50 and a product of 576. Find them.
- Two numbers have a sum of 50 and a difference of 15. Find them.
- Three consecutive numbers have a product of 5814. Find them.

I am sure that you can see that, with a bit of imagination and a creative approach, the possibilities are endless. These are intended to serve only as examples. The important thing to remember, however, is that pupils must be encouraged to explain and compare the strategies they have used.

Supporting open-ended, investigative activities

There are many examples of much-used open-ended activities that require the use of a calculator. In these sorts of situation the calculator takes care of all the calculations, thus freeing up time for the pupils to concentrate on developing the problem-solving and investigative skills. In Chapter 5, when considering ways of using spreadsheets in mathematics, the activity *MAXBOX* was described. This can be done as a practical, cutting-out and making activity, or in a more abstract fashion, using a calculator, or as a modelling activity on a spreadsheet. The activity will not be repeated here, but turn back to Chapter 5 and refresh your memory. It is an excellent activity, which the pupils will enjoy, and they will also do a lot of valuable problem-solving.

Making predictions and general statements

The importance of providing pupils with opportunities to identify patterns and make predictions was highlighted in the earlier section on fractions and decimals. This theme can be developed further through particular calculator-based investigations. One of my favourites is called *Zoom*. With the aid of a calculator, pupils work their way through the flow diagram shown in Figure 6.1. You could initially do this as a whole-class, teacher-led activity, using an on-screen calculator, with the pupils each using their own pocket-sized version. After a few cycles through the flow diagram, ask everyone to stop when they have pressed the equals key, then discuss what they can see in the calculator display. They should all have the same answer, or a number that is getting closer and closer to that answer, and the answer should be 4. They may be surprised at this, particularly in view of the fact that they all started with a different number at the top of the flow diagram. You could ask them

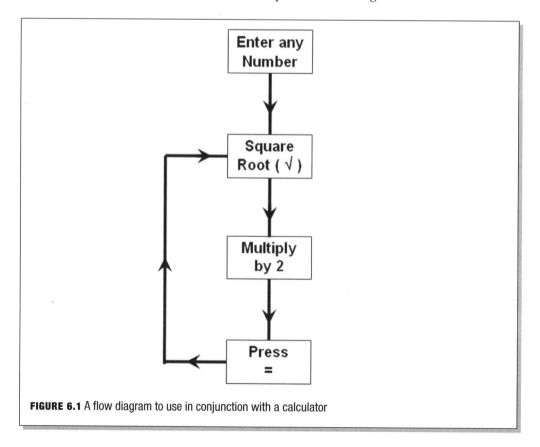

FIGURE 6.1 A flow diagram to use in conjunction with a calculator

all to try it again, using another starting number, to see what happens this time. Again, the answers should all be converging or 'zooming in' on an answer of 4. Now give time for the pupils to investigate further on their own. Instead of multiplying by 2 in the flow diagram, tell them to multiply by 3 and see what happens this time. They could also try multiplying by 4, 5 and 6. Can they spot a connection between the number they multiply by each time and the number the calculator zooms in on? During plenary discussions you could ask pupils to predict what would happen if they multiplied by 10, or 11, or 12 and to make a general statement about the multiplier and the answer. Equipping pupils to make these sorts of prediction and general statements is the whole purpose of this activity and will be reflected in the learning objectives for the lesson.

Summary

Having worked your way through this chapter and, hopefully, tried some of the suggested activities, you will appreciate that:

- A calculator is a powerful and efficient tool, but we should not allow children to use it as a substitute for answering simple arithmetic problems that can be done mentally or using pencil and paper methods. Children should only use it as a calculating tool when they are dealing with relatively complex calculations at the upper end of Key Stage 2.
- The calculator can, however, be used by pupils throughout Key Stage 2 as a checking tool and as a way of exploring the number system, place value, properties of numbers and fractions and decimals.
- The calculator can also be used by the teacher to demonstrate a range of mathematical concepts to pupils of all ages, including those in Key Stage 1.
- Being able to use a calculator effectively involves:
  - knowing the technicalities of how to use the calculator and how to interpret the results that it displays
  - knowing when it is appropriate to use a calculator as opposed to using mental or pencil and paper methods
  - the ability to approximate and estimate in order to check that answers displayed are reasonable.
- In order to get the most out of an electronic calculator you need to know how to use it correctly. These are important skills that most pupils will not pick up on their own and therefore need to be taught in a direct way. This means that the main focus of some of the mathematics lessons that you teach will be the technicalities of using a calculator.

- In order to teach your pupils how to use the facilities offered by a calculator, first you need to know how to use one yourself.

References and additional reading

DfEE (1998) *The Implementation of the National Numeracy Strategy: The Final Report of the Numeracy Task Force*. London: DfEE.

DfEE (1999) *Framework for teaching mathematics from Reception to Year 6*. London: DfEE.

Ofsted (2000) *The National Numeracy Strategy: The First Year*. London: Ofsted.

Ofsted (2002) *The Teaching of Calculation in Primary Schools*. London: Ofsted.

SCAA (1997) *The Use of Calculators at Key Stages 1 to 3 (Discussion Paper Number 9)*. London: SCAA.

Using ICT in mathematics in Foundation Stage

Introduction

The general approach adopted so far in this book has been to examine broad organisational approaches to using ICT in the teaching of mathematics, for example the use of interactive whiteboards, the use of one computer to support whole-class teaching and the use of computers by pupils in the classroom or computer suite. Almost without exception, these broad approaches can be embraced by teachers working in Foundation Stage to enhance the teaching of mathematics. For example, there are many software packages, both general and subject-specific, together with web-based resources, that are suitable for use on an interactive whiteboard with very young children. Similarly, a single computer, even without the luxury of an interactive whiteboard, can be used effectively to promote interactions with the whole class, because the pupils are physically small, enabling them to gather around the screen easily. Examples of how the computer can be used to support data-handling in Foundation Stage will be discussed later in this chapter. The pupils themselves can use the computers, typically in the classroom, but possibly in a computer suite or other dedicated area. This will assist their mathematical development in areas such as sorting, matching, patterning, number recognition, counting, comparing, ordering, sequencing, shape recognition and general spatial awareness. As well as focusing on the mathematics, these computer-based experiences, using keyboards and mice, provide young pupils with vital opportunities to address aspects of their physical development such as hand–eye coordination. Finally, even calculators, as discussed in the previous chapter, have a place in the Foundation Stage classroom, particularly when pupils are engaged in role-play which uses a range of everyday technology. The use of ICT in role-play will be considered in greater detail later.

So, if all that has gone before is equally applicable to Foundation Stage, why have a separate chapter? First, because it enables me to emphasise the fact that ICT is not the exclusive domain of Key Stages 1 and 2, and second, because it is in Foundation Stage that ICT can be interpreted and exemplified in its broadest sense.

Much of what has been discussed earlier has revolved around the use of computers but, in this chapter, you will see that ICT incorporates a much wider range of technology such as programmable toys, audio equipment, digital cameras and other everyday electronic gadgets. All of these can be put to good effect in Foundation Stage, but it is also worth noting that much of it can also be used with older children, even those in Key Stage 2.

Data-handling with computers in Foundation Stage

In Chapter 4 it was suggested that, with a creative approach, one computer can be used to provide meaningful data-handling activities for whole classes of pupils. You might recall that the vital ingredient in such activities is the initial discussions that develop as a result of the question or issue raised by the teacher. Two examples were described in detail to illustrate the procedure, one aimed at Key Stage 1 and the other at Key Stage 2. A further example, suitable for Foundation Stage, will be discussed here.

With the children gathered around on the carpet, tell the pupils that you want to find out as much interesting information about them as you can. Ask them what sorts of thing they could tell you about themselves and record these ideas on the board or flipchart. Your list of suggestions might include their name, their age, their hair colour, eye colour, favourite pet, and so on. A data-handling package that is ideally suited to very young pupils is *Pick-a-Picture*, published by BlackCat Educational Software. It uses a set of pre-written templates that allow you to do computer-based data-handling activities very easily. On the computer screen, display 'Ourselves' as a new topic and tell the children that the computer wants to know all about them as well. Compare the information on the list compiled previously with the headings on the computer screen (see Figure 7.1).

Using one of the children as an example, demonstrate how to enter information onto the computer by clicking on each heading and selecting the appropriate option. The child's name can also be typed in. If there are not many children in the group they could come to the front, one by one, and enter their own information in a similar fashion. If you think this is going to take a considerable amount of time it could be done on an individual basis, perhaps with adult support but without the rest of the class watching and becoming restless. Another possible intermediate stage would be to print out the screen-shot shown in Figure 7.1 (*Pick-a-Picture* does this at the click of a button) and make a copy for each child to fill in by hand. They could tick the boy or girl, shade an eye in the appropriate colour, write their age in the box, draw their hair the appropriate length, tick the right or left hand, and so on. After completing the sheet, each child could enter the information onto the computer.

When the data file is complete you could use it to stimulate valuable discussion with the whole class. Display a particular child's information on the screen and ask

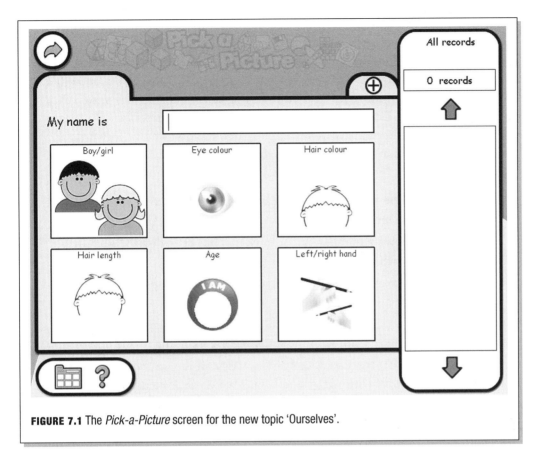

FIGURE 7.1 The *Pick-a-Picture* screen for the new topic 'Ourselves'.

questions such as, *'What is this person's name?'* and *'What colour are his eyes?'*. You could also ask questions that involve simple counting, such as, *'How many children have blonde hair?'*, either by viewing all of the records or possibly in conjunction with the graphing facility, which can display bar charts or pictograms.

Logo-related activities

Computer-based Logo activities were discussed in Chapter 5, but these are really only appropriate for pupils in Key Stage 2 and the top end of Key Stage 1. To prepare pupils for these activities it is essential to provide them with Logo-related experiences during Foundation Stage and Key Stage 1. One of the problems with Logo is that the turtle moves around on a surface (i.e. the computer screen) that is vertical, in stark contrast to the horizontal surface upon which pupils are accustomed to moving around themselves in their everyday lives. This mismatch between the Logo screen and the real world often results in errors and misunderstandings, most noticeably when the turtle is moving down the screen and then has to be instructed to turn right or left. Pupils commonly confuse right and left because they have to be reversed when the turtle is travelling down the screen. So, instead of rushing pupils on to using computer-based Logo programs, we should be providing them with lots of experience in instructing electronic turtles and other programmable toys to move around on the same horizontal surface which they themselves live upon. Commonly used examples of such resources include *Roamer* and *Pixie*. Both have keypads with keys to instruct the toy to move forwards and backwards, and to turn right and left, enabling pupils to explore mathematical activities such as:

- moving the turtle forwards or backwards to stop on a particular spot, marked on the floor with a piece of card or chalk
- moving up and down a number line or track that has been devised such that the numbers are each one unit of movement apart
- guiding the turtle around a treasure map drawn on a large square grid with the size of the squares corresponding to one unit of movement
- using the turtle in conjunction with giant versions of number track games such as snakes and ladders, again with the squares corresponding to one unit of movement
- manoeuvring the turtle through a simple maze or obstacle course.

Another valuable experience for young children, which perhaps ought to come before they start to use the likes of *Roamer* and *Pixie*, is to play with radio-controlled cars and toys. These feature strongly on children's Christmas and birthday present wish-lists and so you could be forgiven for thinking that they are merely toys with little or no educational value. However, under the guidance of a skilled adult, children can not only derive great pleasure from these toys, but also develop an understanding of the mathematical language associated with position and movement as well as valuable social skills.

So, by providing pupils with opportunities to play with programmable turtles and radio-controlled toys, you are addressing key aspects of their mathematical and social development such as:

- being able to listen to and give instructions
- being able to work as part of a group and take turns
- developing an understanding of the language associated with position and movement
- understanding the distinction between different types of movement, that is, forwards or backwards movement as opposed to turning
- being able to use number names and symbols correctly

■ being able to count reliably and accurately

■ developing generic skills such as problem-solving, estimation, and trial and improvement.

Now that is an awful lot of learning from things that many people would consider to be toys!

Using audio tapes, CDs and multimedia

For as long as anyone can remember, effective teachers have provided opportunities for young children to share and enjoy songs, rhymes and poems to assist language, mathematical and social development. Here are just a few that I can recall.

'One, two, buckle my shoe'
'1, 2, 3, 4, 5, once I caught a fish alive'
'This old man, he played one, he played knick-knack on my thumb'
'One man went to mow, went to mow a meadow'
'Ten green bottles hanging on the wall'
'Ten fat sausages, sizzling in a pan'
'There were ten in a bed and the little one said "Roll over, roll over"'
'Five little speckled frogs, sat on a speckled log'
'Five currant buns in a baker's shop'
'Five little ducks went swimming one day'

For many years, songs and rhymes of this type have been available on audio cassettes, enabling the teacher to play them to the children, complete with musical accompaniment, before the children join in themselves. A more recent development is the use of audio CDs that allow the teacher to jump instantly to any song, instead of having to play them in linear fashion or endure the rather hit-and-miss approach of fast-forwarding and rewinding the tape. To make the best possible use of these resources, they ought to be accompanied by other visual aids such as number lines, number tracks and flashcards displaying words and numbers, so that the children can make the link between the sounds they are hearing and the associated words and number symbols. There are also opportunities to address aspects of the children's physical development when reciting these songs and rhymes, by building in movement around the classroom, the formation of groups, getting them to stand up and down, asking them to show hands and fingers, and so on.

The important linking of visual aids to counting songs and rhymes has, to some extent, been taken care of by the latest technological developments in the field of multimedia. Now children can experience and enjoy CD-ROMs, computer software and web-based resources that literally are all-singing and all-dancing, and incorporate words and number symbols synchronised with the sound so that each word is highlighted at the appropriate moment in time.

Using everyday technology in role-play

The 'home corner' has always been a feature of Foundation Stage and some Key Stage 1 classrooms but nowadays teachers need to look beyond the home when providing role-play settings for young children. It is not uncommon to see children now experiencing the supermarket, the bank, the library, the post office and the doctor's surgery, all within the confines of the classroom. In all of these real-world settings children are experiencing technology and so we must prepare them for this in their role-playing activities. By using some of the latest resources, which imitate a range of everyday technology, we can facilitate young children's learning about their world in a safe but realistic way. These resources include:

- electronic calculators with chunky keys and a large display to help children to familiarise themselves with the way that numbers appear electronically
- shopping tills with electronic displays and the facility to use a large swipe card
- cash dispensers that require a code to be typed in before plastic coins are issued
- mobile phones with numbered keys and electronic displays
- weighing scales with simple digital readouts
- microwave ovens and other domestic appliances with numbered dials, electronic displays and countdown facilities.

As well as providing important opportunities to develop key mathematical concepts such as number recognition, counting and the language associated with comparing, ordering and sequencing, these sorts of activity play a vital role in the children's personal and social development in using their imagination, expressing their thoughts and feelings, their interactions with one another and their knowledge and understanding of the world.

Digital cameras in Foundation Stage

Digital cameras could have been included in the above list of everyday technology that young children should be experiencing in their role-playing. However, they will be considered separately because they offer much potential for both children and teachers. Pairs and small groups of children, with adult assistance, could use a digital still or video camera to record everyday features that are of mathematical interest. These could be within the classroom, around the school, outside in the school grounds, within the local town or village, or at the venue of a school trip or visit. In terms of the mathematics, the interest could be in such things as different 2-D and 3-D shapes with which the pupils are familiar, symmetry, repeating patterns, number symbols, collections of objects that can be counted or sorted later, scenes involving money, items that can be compared and ordered in terms of size, and so on. Not only will the children enjoy taking photographs and videoing these every-day scenes, but they can also be used as the focus of some valuable discussion with the whole class to explore key mathematical topics. You could also use a digital camera yourself, as part of your preparation and planning, to record everyday scenes that are of mathematical interest and can be shared with the children.

Another mathematical concept that can be clarified by the use of digital cameras is time. Not only do young children find it difficult to tell the time, but they also have problems understanding the concept of time and the way that everyday events are sequenced. Photographs or short video clips could be used to illustrate common events in a child's typical daily routine. These could be shown to the children, discussed and then sequenced. Not only will this help children to develop an understanding of the passage of time, but it will also provide opportunities to introduce and reinforce important language associated with ordering and sequencing events.

Summary

All of the approaches suggested in Chapters 2 to 6 are relevant to and can be adapted for Foundation Stage settings. In addition, this chapter has illustrated that Foundation Stage offers a huge potential for using a comprehensive range of ICT equipment other than computers and calculators. As well as being wide-ranging in terms of the resources, the suggested approaches presented in this chapter also demonstrate how, at this vital first stage of a child's schooling, it is more than just mathematical development that concerns us. By using ICT creatively in the teaching of mathematics at Foundation Stage, we are also addressing key aspects of children's physical, personal, social, emotional and language development as well as their knowledge and understanding of the world around them. This is, of course, true of any phase of education but, in these early years of education, when children are developing so rapidly, it is critical that we focus on the 'whole child', not just the mathematics.

References and additional reading

QCA (2000) *Curriculum Guidance for the Foundation Stage*. London: Qualifications and Curriculum Authority. Mathematical Development section, pp. 68–81. Details of this publication are also available at: http://www.qca.org.uk/223.html

Web resources

Pick-a-Picture is available from BlackCat Educational Software: http://www.blackcatsoftware.com/

Pixie is available from Swallow Systems: http://www.swallow.co.uk/

Roamer and *RoamerWorld* are available from Valiant Technology: http://www.valiant-technology.com/

Using ICT to support out-of-school mathematics

Introduction

Having to do maths homework has become a way of life, even for pupils in primary schools, but I wonder if its announcement by the teacher is accompanied by the same moans and groans as it was in days gone by? Do children today look upon homework as a penance in the same way as their parents did, or are we now being more creative in the ways that we embrace out-of-school learning, so that it is both enjoyable and beneficial? We shall see.

I am sure we all remember homework in the traditional mould: issued on a particular day of the week, handed in the next, marked by the teacher, and returned in time for the next thrilling instalment later in the week. Most teachers set homework only because they felt obliged to, because maths appeared on the school's homework timetable (sometimes twice!), and they loathed it as much as the pupils did because of all the marking that it generated. But the marks were meaningless anyway because, let's face it, most pupils copied from one another on the bus on the way to school. The role of the parent was an interesting one: enrolled by the school to act as homework policeman on its behalf, trained to say things like, 'Get up to your room and don't come down until you've done your homework!' and to sign the homework diary to confirm that the allotted time had been spent. Hands up all those who can remember maths homework like that.

In the late 1980s, Ruth Merttens, a lecturer in what was then the Polytechnic of North London, started a project that aimed to break away from this traditional approach to maths homework. The Involving Mathematics for Parents, Children and Teachers (IMPACT) Project initially involved only about a dozen primary schools in North London but, within a few years, it expanded both nationally and internationally to include thousands of schools in the UK, as well as the US and Canada. The project was based on the premise that, in relation to maths (and indeed all other subjects), parents want to know the answers to two questions: *What is my child doing in maths?* and *How is he or she getting on?* What better way is there to discover the answers to these questions than to be actively involved in the child's maths work? Promoting this sort of parental involvement was precisely what the IMPACT Project was all about. Teachers would provide activities for pupils to take home to do with their parents but, instead of merely supervising the work, parents were encouraged to discuss the mathematics and collaborate with their child. The sorts of activity that pupils and their parents typically carried out together included maths games and puzzles, sorting and classifying, measuring, gathering data, drawing and making mathematical shapes, and so on. Teachers were also advised to make the most of the valuable interaction between parent and child in the home, by designing follow-up activities for the pupils to carry out in the classroom. In this way, the work at home was portrayed as being an integral component of the pupils' mathematical learning. This way of working also strengthened home–school links and provided opportunities to invite parents in to school to listen to informative talks about the project, and to participate in mathematical workshops led by staff.

The principle of encouraging pupils and their parents to engage in mathematics together was embraced by a number of publishers in the 1990s, including Scholastic, which published a range of IMPACT Maths books covering all aspects of primary mathematics. Letts Educational also promoted this theme with separate homework books for Key Stages 1, 2 and 3, each one presenting a range of maths activities but always with an 'Ask the Family' section to encourage collaborative work in the home.

The aim of this chapter is to explore the issue of mathematics learning outside of normal school hours but with a particular emphasis on the role of ICT. Specific resources, approaches and sources of further advice will be suggested, but first there are a couple of key issues that need to be discussed.

Key issues to consider

Is homework important?

The traditional model of maths homework, as described above does raise doubts about the value of inflicting it upon pupils and, to some extent, the teachers who have to organise, manage and assess the work. The government has no doubts at all about the value of homework, stating that:

> Research over a number of years in this and other countries has shown that homework can make an important contribution to pupils' progress at school... [and] ...there is evidence that pupils in the highest achieving schools spend more time on learning activities at home than pupils in other schools.
>
> (DfEE 1998)

More recently, and specifically in relation to mathematics, the government states in its National Numeracy Strategy documentation (DfEE 1999) that:

> Homework supports the development of independent learning skills, and provides parents with an opportunity to take part in their children's education.

and that:

> better numeracy standards occur when
>
> ■ parents are kept well-informed and encouraged to be involved through discussions at school and sometimes in work with pupils at home
>
> ■ there is a daily, dedicated mathematics lesson in every class, with lesson time extended through out-of-class activities and regular homework

There would appear to be no evidence to suggest that simply spending more time doing maths at home in itself has a direct impact on attainment, but a recurring theme in most discussions about the value of homework is the active involvement of parents. To anyone who is directly involved in, or has a sound understanding of, child development, this observation should be obvious. Children benefit from generous doses of support, encouragement and praise, and this can be administered particularly effectively by their parents. Children are more likely to have a positive attitude to learning if they can see that their education is valued by their parents. Children learn through discussion, interaction and collaboration with others and, again, the catalyst for this sort of cooperative learning can be their parents. So the importance of doing work at home is not so much in the mathematics itself but more in the personal interactions, processes, attitudes and values that it can promote. The good news is that maths homework which uses ICT fits this model of social constructivism extremely well, as we shall see later in this chapter.

Equality of opportunity

As soon as teachers consider devising activities to be completed by pupils at home that require the use of computers or other ICT resources, it raises a number of equal opportunity issues, often referred to in phrases such as 'the digital divide' or 'the haves and the have-nots'. A recent government publication (BECTA 2005) succinctly confirms what most people intuitively know already when it states that:

> Access to and use of ICT at home varies with socio-economic group. Lower socio-economic groups are currently relatively disadvantaged.

Despite the fact that the price of equipping the home with a computer has fallen considerably in recent years, it still represents a significant financial investment and so schools ought not to be providing an education for their pupils that is based on the assumption that they will have access to a home computer. I don't think anyone can legitimately argue against this view.

However, there is an increasing proportion of pupils who do have access to these valuable resources at home and so it would be unwise to disregard the potential on offer. Government survey statistics (BECTA 2002, 2003) indicate that the proportion of primary school pupils with access to a computer at home rose from 69 per cent in 2001 to 75 per cent in 2002. This upward trend has almost certainly continued since the 2002 survey, corresponding with an increase in the proportion of children in Key Stage 2 reporting that they use a computer to do homework, from seven per cent in 2001 to forty per cent in 2002 (BECTA 2005). However, despite the increasing availability of computers in the home, the original question still remains: *What do we do about those pupils without access to computers?* There are a number of key approaches and initiatives that teachers and schools could adopt to help them at least make a start in tackling this problem.

Auditing home provision

The first stage in addressing the issue of 'the haves and the have-nots' should be to find out who they are, but I suspect that doing this is the exception rather than the rule. Why not, either as part of a whole-school policy or informally in the classroom with a quick show of hands, find out which pupils have access to computers at home? This will inform the school, or the individual teacher, as to the viability of particular out-of-school maths activities that require the use of ICT. It will also determine the subsequent scale of any remedial measures that the school might like to implement.

Using school computers out-of-hours

One strategy that can help to address the inequality of access to computers is to make the school's facilities available to pupils, their parents and the wider community during out-of-school hours. Individual schools will have invested tens of thousands of pounds equipping the computer suite but, typically, it is used for a relatively small proportion of the week. Unless schools are making use of the facilities during maths and literacy lessons, which typically take place in the morning, then they are likely to be in use for no more than a couple of hours each day. That is a small return on a substantial investment, particularly in view of the rapid rate at which computers depreciate and become obsolete. So why not offer pupils and parents the opportunity to use the computer suite as part of an after-school homework club initiative, or provide workshops for parents who have little or no experience of using ICT? Yes, there will be range of organisational and logistical issues to resolve, but at least consider the possibility and the benefits it will bring in terms of developing home–school links. Many schools have embraced this approach, with the proportion of primary schools making computing facilities available to pupils out of normal school hours growing from 44 per cent in 2002 to 55 per cent in 2004 (DfES 2004).

Computer loan schemes

As has already been stated on a number of occasions in this book, computers are an expensive investment but, despite this, many schools have put in place loan schemes to help address the equality of opportunity issue. A government survey conducted in 2004 revealed that six per cent of primary schools had such a scheme. With the price of computers continuing to fall and with an increasing number of schools looking to establish creative commercial sponsorship schemes, this proportion is likely to expand in the future. A charitable organisation, the e-Learning Foundation, provides just one example of how attempts are being made to reduce the effect of the 'digital divide'. The Foundation was established in 2001 and has been working with schools, parents, local businesses and the public sector to ensure that all pupils have access to the ICT learning resources that they need, both at home and at school.

Maths out of school with a computer

The preceding discussions have established that homework, particularly when it uses ICT, does not necessarily have to be completed in the home. Homework clubs in school or elsewhere offer alternative venues but, for simplicity's sake, the term 'homework' will continue to be used here. Assuming that the equality of opportunity issue has been resolved and a belief in the value of doing homework has been fostered, the next step is to consider what sorts of approach should be considered when devising maths homework activities that use ICT. In broad terms a twofold distinction can be made between homework activities that *definitely* require the use of ICT and those that *could* involve ICT if the pupil so chooses.

Activities that require the use of ICT

If you are going to provide these sorts of activity then you need to ensure that the equality of opportunity issue has been addressed scrupulously. Assuming it has, this opens up a huge range of possibilities for pupils doing maths homework with a computer. Essentially, all of the strategies and approaches discussed in Chapter 5, *Teaching mathematics in the computer suite*, can be considered again but now in terms of a different venue for the learning experience. There are, however, a number of key issues that need to be examined closely.

First, the pupils will not have the luxury of your explanations, guidance and support whilst working at home, and you will need to ensure that homework tasks are clear so that they can be carried out independently. Depending on the activity, this will require a combination, in varying degrees, of carefully designed handouts and explanatory discussions in the classroom. On some occasions you might also want to build in a collaborative dimension so that pupils have to discuss and explain the activity to an adult at home, but never assume that the adult will be a substitute for you in terms of mathematical knowledge and understanding of the task.

The second key issue relates to the availability of software in the home. It is unlikely that the licences for the commercial software that pupils use at school extend to cover home use. There may be rare examples where this is the case and so you can arrange for the pupils to take home a floppy disk or CD-ROM, but this is the exception rather than the rule. Another possibility offered by some publishers is the purchase of educational software by parents at heavily discounted rates. One publisher that offers such a scheme is SoftEase. Again, this raises the issue of equality of opportunity and it would be wholly inappropriate to expect all parents to purchase software to support their children's learning at home. The solution to this problem of software access is to use resources that are free, which in most cases means accessing websites on the internet or downloading free software. Yes, well spotted: yet another example of equality of opportunity. Just because there is a computer at home does not necessarily mean that there is internet access, although in the vast majority of cases there is. Nevertheless, this is another question to be asking when you are conducting your initial audits of home provision and to be considering when devising your homework activities.

With the numerous equality of opportunity issues addressed, you can now start to think about the sorts of task you could get your pupils to do out of school with a computer. Here are just a few possibilities.

The Interactive Teaching Programs

The ITPs have been discussed at length in Chapter 2, in relation to their being used by the teacher on an interactive whiteboard, and again in Chapter 5 in terms of pupils using them at the computer. The important points to stress here are first, that all of these resources are free; second, they can be accessed and used as web pages via a live internet connection; and finally, they can be downloaded for use later when perhaps there is no internet access. All of the suggestions made in Chapter 5 could be adapted to form the basis of homework activities and with a creative approach you could come up with many additional activities of your own.

The *Using ICT to Support Mathematics* CD-ROM programs

Chapter 4 described how this suite of programs can be used by pupils working at a computer. Like the ITPs above, all of the programs are free and can be accessed as web pages or downloaded for use later. They could be used as the basis of homework activities for pupils of all ages and there is much potential for parental involvement. For example, *Toy Shop* is a two-player strategy game that a child and parent could play together.

The *Easter School* CD-ROM programs

This suite of five programs was also described in Chapter 4. They can be freely downloaded and installed for use later, when perhaps there is no live internet connection. The programs are designed for use by pupils at Key Stage 2 and cover aspects of mathematics including mental skills, angles, estimation and problem-solving. They are ideally suited for homework activities.

Logo activities

The importance of using Logo to support the mathematics curriculum was considered in Chapter 5. Logo work at school could be reinforced and practised at home. Software availability on home computers is not a problem because one of the most popular Logo packages used in primary schools is available as a free download on the internet: *MSW Logo*, published by Softronix. Many primary schools choose to use this program because it is free but, even if an alternative is used for school-based Logo activities, there is no reason why *MSW Logo* could not be used at home because, generally speaking, there is great consistency in the Logo commands from one program to another.

Spreadsheet activities

Suggestions as to how pupils can use spreadsheets to explore a range of mathematical areas were provided in Chapter 5. All of these activities could be adapted or extended to make them suitable for homework. The only issue would be the availability of a spreadsheet program on home computers although, rather like Logo, one package is much like another and so it is not essential that pupils use precisely the same spreadsheet at school and at home. The spreadsheet skills introduced and developed at school should be easily transferable to an alternative version at home, but this assumes that an alternative is, in fact, available. Thankfully, there are a number of free spreadsheet programs that can be downloaded from the internet and installed on pupils' computers at home, for example the *Sphygmic Software Spreadsheet*.

SATs revision and practice

The routine consolidation and practice of basic maths skills is a common theme for homework activities and there are many web-based resources that facilitate this. Sadly, with all the pressures associated with performance tables, the focus is often on preparation for national tests, but one hopes that most of the time the driving force is the desire for children to learn mathematics rather than simply teaching to the test. There are some priced services available, to which schools can subscribe, for example *SAM Learning*. Typically, schools are provided with usernames and passwords to distribute to pupils to enable them to log on, either at school or at home. A simple management system is sometimes available to staff which provides information about pupils' levels of activity on the system, such as frequency and duration of use, as well as performance. In addition to these subscription services there are numerous free websites that offer similar revision and practice facilities, one of the better examples being the BBC's *ReviseWise*, which is aimed at pupils in Key Stage 2.

Other web-based resources

In addition to the web-based resources aimed specifically at revision and practice for national tests, there are many others that could be used by pupils of all ages and abilities as the basis of maths homework activities. Some of these are subscription services, for example *GridClub* and *AtSchool*, whereas others, provided by organisations such as the BBC and Research Machines, are completely free.

Activities that could use ICT

These sorts of activity provide a possible solution to the equality of opportunity issue. If you feel that you have not addressed this crucial issue fully, then avoid activities for which computer access is a prerequisite and, instead, devise alternatives that offer the potential to use such facilities but can also be tackled successfully, using more traditional approaches. For example, those pupils with access to a computer could word-process their work instead of writing it, carry out a number investigation using a spreadsheet instead of a calculator, produce graphs using a data-handling package instead of drawing them by hand, create a symmetrical pattern using drawing or painting software instead of using pencil and paper, and so on. A key consideration must be to ensure that those pupils without access to a computer are not disadvantaged in terms of either the amount of time the traditional approach requires or the assessment of the finished product. We don't want a situation whereby some pupils are spending considerably longer on their work than others and are being penalised for the quality of presentation, just because they did not have access to a computer. You might need to think very carefully about this sort of differentiation in contrast to, and possibly in addition to, differentiation according to ability. Perhaps those pupils with computer access could be required to do more of whatever is being done or asked to do it in a slightly different way. If you are creative you can turn this situation to your advantage by exploring the possibility of comparing and contrasting the different approaches that the two groups adopt. Make a point of explaining and discussing the two alternative approaches to the homework at the time you are setting it and then, after they have completed it, discuss the pupils' contrasting experiences. This reiterates two issues that have already been raised in this chapter. First, there is the need to establish which pupils do and do not have access to computers at home, and second, there is the importance of integrating homework activities into what takes place in the classroom, even if this is only by way of a brief discussion of what the pupils have done.

Summary

This chapter has identified some of the key issues that schools must take into account if they are successfully to exploit the benefits offered by pupils engaging in mathematics outside normal school hours. A range of approaches, activities and resources has also been provided in order to get you started on the road to designing creative homework for your pupils. The main themes which permeate the foregoing discussions are:

- The importance of addressing equality of opportunity issues in terms of access to computers, access to the internet and access to software. With regard to access to the wide range of free software described in this chapter, one possibility to consider is the production of a CD-ROM containing all of the free downloads that you want your pupils and their parents to make use of at home. Copies of the CD-ROM could then be taken home and all the software installed without the need for internet access.

- The need for homework to be set for all the right reasons. It needs to be valued by teachers, pupils and parents and, therefore, needs to have a clear purpose and be an integral part of the mathematics learning, sitting alongside the work that is done in school.

- The vital role played by parents when it comes to the issue of homework. This should not be merely a policing role. Activities should be devised to encourage parents to interact and work collaboratively with their children, so that they can all learn and talk about mathematics together. Homework can also be used as a vehicle to strengthen home–school links by inviting groups of parents into school to discuss approaches to cooperative learning with their children and to engage in hands-on workshop sessions, using the school's ICT facilities.

References and additional reading

BECTA (2002) *Young People and ICT 2001: Findings from a Survey Conducted in Autumn 2001*. Coventry: BECTA. This publication is also available at: http://www.partners.becta.org.uk

BECTA (2003) *Young People and ICT 2002: Findings from a Survey Conducted in Autumn 2002*. Coventry: BECTA. This publication is also available at: http://www.partners.becta.org.uk

BECTA (2005) *The Becta Review 2005: Evidence on the Progress of ICT in Education*. Coventry: BECTA. This publication is also available at: http://www.partners.becta.org.uk

DfEE (1998) *Homework: Guidelines for Primary and Secondary Schools*. London: DfEE. This publication is also available at: http://www.dfes.gov.uk/homework/contents.shtml

DfEE (1999) *The National Numeracy Strategy: Framework for Teaching Mathematics*. London: DfEE. This publication is also available at: http://www.standards.dfes.gov.uk/primary/mathematics/

DfES (2004) *ICT in Schools Survey 2004*. London: DfES. This publication is also available at: http://www.partners.becta.org.uk

Web resources

Further details of the work of the e-Learning Foundation can be found at: http://www.e-learningfoundation.com/

SoftEase sells parent licences for most of its products: http://www.softease.com/

The Interactive Teaching Programs (ITPs) are available in the mathematics section of the Primary National Strategy website: http://www.standards.dfes.gov.uk/primary/mathematics/

The *Using ICT to Support Mathematics in Primary Schools* software is available at: http://www.standards.dfes.gov.uk/primary/publications/mathematics/using_ict_in_maths/

The *Easter School CD-ROM* software is available at: http://www.standards.dfes.gov.uk/primary/publications/mathematics/12816/

MSW Logo is published by Softronix and can be downloaded from: http://www.softronix.com/

The *Sphygmic Software Spread*sheet can be downloaded from: http://www.ds.unifi.it/stefanin/AGR_2001/SH/sssheet.htm

SAM Learning offers a web-based subscription service that includes materials for Key Stages 1 and 2: http://www.samlearning.com/

The BBC's *ReviseWise* website is aimed at pupils in Key Stage 2 and is free: http://www.bbc.co.uk/schools/revisewise/

GridClub is a web-based subscription service aimed at primary pupils: http://www.gridclub.com/

AtSchool is a web-based subscription service with sections for Key Stages 1 and 2 and Early Years: http://www.atschool.co.uk/

The BBC offers a wide range of web-based maths resources suitable for pupils in primary schools: http://www.bbc.co.uk/schools/4_11/numeracy.shtml

The *Pathways* section of Research Machines' *Learning Alive* website has links to a range of useful maths resources: http://www.learningalive.co.uk/pathways/

The *Parents Information Network* provides a wide range of guidance on computers and education for parents of children of toddler age through to 18: http://www.pin.org.uk/

There is a section of the government's Standards Site which provides parents with advice on helping their children with numeracy: http://www.mathsyear2000.org/standards/

DfES ParentsCentre: http://www.parentscentre.gov.uk

Looking forward, looking back

Looking back

When embarking on this project I took the advice of Julie Andrews and started at the very beginning, a very good place to start, and consequently the first chapter was the first to be written. The months that have since elapsed represent a considerable timespan in terms of the continual lightning advances that are being made in the technological world. The cutting-edge examples of ICT use described in the opening pages are almost certainly more widespread as I write this final chapter, and may even be commonplace by the time you read this. The most recent reports from government bodies confirm that progress continues to be made with regard to the use of ICT in primary schools, particularly in mathematics (Ofsted 2005a, 2005b). Schools have acquired more ICT resources, particularly interactive whiteboards, than ever before, teachers and pupils are making greater use of what is available and the overall quality of what is going on is steadily improving. However, there continues to be a number of areas where there is room for improvement. For example, many teachers are beginning to make effective use of interactive whiteboards themselves when working with the whole class, but are not extending this into group and independent work later in the lesson. There is, therefore, much potential for the pupils to use the interactive whiteboard at times when it would otherwise be idle. Another example, this time at the whole-school level, concerns headteachers, who need to monitor teachers' use of ICT in order to judge whether it is enhancing teaching and learning and helping to raise standards. It is all very well having more in the way of ICT resources and using them to a greater extent, but how are they impacting on standards in mathematics? The issues of 'impact' and 'cause and effect' are difficult to tackle, but schools and LEAs are better equipped with statistical information than ever before to at least make a start on justifying the vast amounts of money that have been invested in ICT and the associated support structures. The case for using ICT was presented in the second part of Chapter 1. Now what is needed is for individual schools to add to this body of evidence by demonstrating that what teachers are doing with ICT is making a real difference to children's learning.

Based on my own recent observations of what is happening in primary schools, I feel that one of the biggest issues that needs to be addressed is the great variability regarding the effective use of ICT in mathematics. Despite the promising signs noted by Ofsted and the pockets of real excellence that undoubtedly exist, there remains a significant proportion of teachers and schools that, for a variety of reasons, is being left behind. This is sometimes due to lack of resources, as indicated by the results of a recent survey in which 43 per cent of primary teachers reported that lack of access to classroom computers hinders their use of ICT, and 33 per cent expressed concerns about the lack of access to an interactive whiteboard (BESA 2006). However, at the same time there are teachers who do have access to classroom computers and interactive whiteboards but are simply not using them, other than in purely superficial ways. This could be due to lack of training and support in how to use the technology or it could be a lack of awareness of the potential being offered. Sadly, there are also a very small number of teachers out there who are determined not to use ICT in their teaching and are prepared to find any excuse to accomplish this. Even for those who are using ICT extensively, the key issue is one of *quality* and *effectiveness* rather than merely frequency and duration, and the root of the problem is more to do with mathematics than the technology. Teachers who are both knowledgeable and skilful with regard to ICT may lack an understanding of the nature of mathematics and how children learn. Children learn mathematics by experimenting, speculating, discovering, questioning, reflecting, explaining and discussing, and so those teachers who see children simply as empty vessels to be filled with factual knowledge are unlikely to be successful, no matter how much they use ICT. I would argue that it is better to teach mathematics using approaches based around all those '-ing' words but without ICT, than to adopt the 'empty vessel' approach using ICT. If you can incorporate all those '-ing' words as well as the ICT then you really will start to make an impact in the classroom.

Looking forward: continued support for the use of ICT

It is likely that the recent expansion in the effective use of ICT noted by Ofsted will continue. Everyone acknowledges that ICT is good for education and so there will be political and financial support for it at all levels and from a range of stakeholders. The government will introduce new initiatives, the private sector will devise innovative ways to provide resources (as long as there's something in it for them), schools will happily spend increasing amounts of money on ICT, teachers and pupils will have greater access to ICT resources and the use of ICT across the curriculum, including mathematics, will become more widespread. But the long-term solution is not simply to pour more money into the educational system, because the technology itself is not going to result in creative approaches to teaching. More important than the money and the technology are the leadership and vision of senior managers in schools who recognise the potential offered by ICT to improve the quality of teaching and learning. On many occasions in recent years I have been able to identify pairs of schools operating under almost identical financial and socio-economic circumstances, but whilst in one school there has been little or no evidence of ICT being utilised, in the other I have observed the creative and innovative use of ICT by the majority of staff across a range of subjects. The crucial factor has invariably been the leadership and vision of the headteacher and other senior managers. Visionary headteachers give priority to ICT in terms of funding for resources, staff training and technical support. They also acknowledge that innovation takes time and so create periods for their staff to reflect on the training they have experienced and to explore the possibilities. They also lead by example, showing a commitment and enthusiasm for ICT that rubs off on their staff. The role of other managers in the school, such as the ICT and maths coordinators, is also crucial. Without this whole-school commitment to ICT, the best we can ever hope for is for individual teachers to beaver away on their own but with limited success due to the lack of support from above.

Looking forward: technological developments

Crystal-ball gazing is very difficult when it comes to technological developments because we simply do not know what lies around the corner. However, it is possible to provide a few examples of recent innovations that illustrate the rapid pace of change and might help us to anticipate what is to come.

The 'Green Machine' is a $100 (approximately £65) laptop which has been designed by researchers at the Massachusetts Institute of Technology, primarily for use in developing countries. It is a relatively low-specification computer but is extremely durable and is powered by a 'wind-up' mechanism similar to that found in the Freeplay radios that have been available in recent years. Although the 'Green Machine' may not find its way into primary classrooms in this country, it does illustrate how basic computing facilities can be provided for every pupil at a relatively low cost. Obviously, at these prices pupils will not have access to an all-singing, all-dancing multimedia machine, but for basic word-processing, data-handling and spreadsheet work a cheap, low-specification computer is sufficient.

Whilst many schools and teachers are still eagerly awaiting delivery of their first interactive whiteboard, there are some who are experiencing a truly portable interactive system that requires no touch-sensitive board at all. A standard digital projector displays its image on any surface and an infrared pen sends a signal to a receiver connected to the computer. The pen is used to calibrate the system, just like a normal interactive whiteboard, and then it is ready to use. These sorts of portable system are targeted at the business person on the move, but they are certainly worthy of consideration for use in schools, not least because they are considerably cheaper than a conventional arrangement as there is no whiteboard to pay for.

Another recent development in the area of interactive presentation technology is that of 'no-shadow' digital projectors. One of the problems with a conventional projector is that the user often casts a shadow on the screen, thus obscuring the material being presented. The latest technology, albeit quite expensive at the moment, uses a system of internal aspheric mirrors to project an image that is always shadow-free. Another feature is that the projector can be placed very close to the board but still produce a large image; at a distance of only 45 cm an image that is 2 metres wide can be projected!

Looking forward: innovative ways of working

Instead of being constantly obsessed with new technology, perhaps we ought to concentrate on working more creatively with the resources that are readily available to us at this moment in time. This philosophy lies at the heart of much of what is proposed in this book. Many of the creative approaches to teaching mathematics that have been discussed in earlier chapters require nothing more than a modestly equipped computer, and so it is the knowledge, skill and imagination of the teacher that will have the greatest impact on the quality of teaching and learning, not the availability of the latest state-of-the-art technology. Continuing with my tentative look into the future, this principle of using what we already have, but to better effect, can be applied to the field of virtual learning environments (VLEs) or 'learning platforms' as they are sometimes known. These VLEs have been used in higher education for a number of years and are essentially a password-protected corner of the internet, which allows members of the community to communicate with one another and to share digital resources. Postgraduate Certificate of Education (PGCE) students at my own institution have been using a VLE called *Merlin* for several years. It allows staff, school mentors and current and former students to communicate with one another via an internal email system, it facilitates discussions and the posting of questions and answers in an exchange area, it provides electronic access to all course documentation and it enables students to submit assignments to staff electronically, to name just a few of its facilities and benefits. An increasing number of schools are starting to look at VLEs as a way of supporting teaching and learning for pupils, both when they are in school and away from it. School websites and intranets are nothing new but, in the past, these have largely been used to promote the school and to inform outsiders as to what the school is all about. If the school website or intranet is extended to become a VLE then it opens up a whole host of creative possibilities. Pupils can have their own 'portfolio' where they store completed work, as well as work in progress, so that it can be accessed by the appropriate member of staff, pupils can work collaboratively on a project before submitting it, teachers can respond to individual questions raised by pupils, parents can be given direct access to the work and activities in which their children are engaging and staff and parents can establish a dialogue to help improve the pupils' learning experience. These are just a few of the possibilities that a carefully managed VLE or learning platform could offer in the future but, in technological terms, it is a realistic possibility right now.

So both now and in the future, a creative approach does not always require the latest cutting-edge technology. Creativity is all about showing flair, imagination and innovation, but at the same time being realistic, doing simple things well and making the most of the sometimes limited resources that we already have at our disposal. So go on – be creative!

References and additional reading

BESA (2006) *Resources in English Schools Survey 2006*. London: BESA. This publication is also available at: http://www.besa.org.uk

Ofsted (2005a) *The Annual Report of Her Majesty's Chief Inspector of Schools 2004/05*. London: Ofsted. This publication is also available at: http://www.ofsted.gov.uk/publications/annualreport0405/

Ofsted (2005b) *Primary National Strategy: An Evaluation of its Impact in Primary Schools 2004/05*. London: Ofsted. This publication is also available at: http://www.ofsted.gov.uk/publications/

Index